ALAN SEMROW

RIPE

Letters

ALAN SEMROW

Copyright © 2018 Alan Semrow

All rights reserved.

ISBN: 9781723761683

Cover Design: Madelline Morgan-Knox
Author Photo: H.M. Gautsch

Cover Emojis: Noto Fonts. Noto is a trademark of Google Inc. Noto fonts are open source. All Noto fonts are published under the SIL Open Font License, Version 1.1.

Versions of these pieces, including "Dear Steak," "Dear Person," Dear Great White Buffalo," "Dear Vocab," among others, have appeared in *Chosen Magazine*.

For George

CONTENTS

DEAR BIRTHDAY GUY 10
DEAR PURPLE DRANK 16
DEAR JET SKI 20
DEAR STALLION 23
DEAR PETER PAN 26
DEAR HOCKEY 29
DEAR KISSER 33
DEAR TWO WEEKS 35
DEAR DESERT GUY 37
DEAR CITY GUY 42
DEAR RYAN GOSLING LOVER 46
DEAR LOBSTER BISQUE 48
DEAR GREAT WHITE BUFFALO 50
DEAR AFTERNOONER 56
DEAR NAPKIN 60
DEAR ALMOST STRANGER 62
DEAR PHOTOGRAPHER 65
DEAR CARD DEALER 67
DEAR ATLANTA GUY 69
DEAR STEAK 70
DEAR CLEAN-CUT 73
DEAR FIRE LIGHTER 75
DEAR SUNSHINE STATE GUY 79
DEAR DADDY 81
DEAR BLONDIE 83
DEAR VOCAB 85
DEAR TRAVELER 88

DEAR GUY FROM COLLEGE 91
DEAR LAWNMOWER 94
DEAR NEIGHBOR 98
DEAR WEEKEND LOVE 102
DEAR MAPLE LEAF 104
DEAR PRETZELS 108
DEAR PERSON 110
DEAR SMILER 115
DEAR PROFESSIONAL 118
DEAR CONVERSATIONALIST 120
DEAR STREAMS 123
DEAR TOUR GUIDE 125
DEAR JET-SETTER 128
DEAR ONLY CHILD 130
DEAR SUNDAY 134
DEAR ATHLETE 137
DEAR FLANNEL 140
DEAR REMINDER 144

DEAR BIRTHDAY GUY

It wasn't easy getting through to you. Before finally being driven over in the Uber, that fine November morning, I may or may not have muttered something to the effect of:

Fuckin' tops these days.

You're right. I needed to chill. But, at the time you came along, in my mind, one disappointment could have caused a downpour on the parade I'd been prancing around in all weekend.

The night before, a group of some of my favorite people in the whole world had taken me out and, the entire time, proved over and over and over again why I was so lucky to have each of them in my life. Mostly, it was humbling—it made me see that I was so much less capable of going above and beyond in the way they did. I'd formed a circle of a rare breed of humans who don't put themselves first.

What did I do to deserve this? When I was younger, that question carried a darker weight.

At exactly 11:55 pm, five minutes before we planned to ring it all in, I left my circle at the bar. By that point in the night, there was a very low chance of topping the joy I felt. Staying out longer and slipping further into excess—that could have only dampened things. The year before you, it had been an education of sorts. Now, I was twenty-six years old and starting to go about things just a little bit differently. Just a little. I'd learned a few lessons.

In the morning, I woke to nothing but a slight hangover and a message from you:

Cuddles?

We'd been playing this game for a while now.

"Yes," I replied. "Yes, please."

It took time and total impatience on my part for us to get the plan in place. You were online. You were offline. Green light. You were showering. No light. Back on. Finally, you were giving me your address. By around nine o'clock, it was officially on. I got ready and dialed the Uber. The driver, a guy probably in his upper thirties, he asked me, "So, what are your plans for such a nice day?"

I explained that I'm meeting an old friend right now. And, after this, I planned to meet others for brunch.

"Well then, happy birthday," he said. "It's a great day for a birthday."

And it was. It was one of those strangely warm November days when the grass is damp and the world is quiet, but the air, it feels refreshing and the sun is still shining bright. It was different from years before. I'd been living in the city almost exactly a year and three months and, quite deeply, I had experienced change. Before this, I spent a year heartbroken, in a lapse of self-imposed exile, in a very small city where I never intended to spend the rest of my life. Here, I managed to make up for what I see as lost time. I met a lot of people. I formed bonds. I found real fondness for a lot of very different men. Mostly, I lived the shit out of that year, and surfaced from it feeling more grateful, more self-assured, more at ease, more accepting—maybe even, dare I say, more patient.

In the lead-up to the move, a friend told me that a new location wouldn't change who I was deep down—that a change of scenery was incapable of changing who a person *really* was. I now can safely call bullshit on that. At twenty-six, I was changed. And today—this day when I met you—I guess, I felt that I deserved to celebrate the fact.

Once the driver parked the Prius, I looked down at my phone screen—just to make sure we were in the place where your directions said I needed to be. The white door opened. It was you standing and waving. A butterfly fluttered down into the pit of my stomach. You looked just like your pictures.

I thanked the driver and ran over to you. I tapped your arm and then got attacked by the dog who, with her rapid and energetic jumping movements, practically pummeled me into the inside wall.

We followed her up the stairs. At the top, I scanned the room and said, "This is a really nice place." You had this urban vibe going on and almost no furniture.

"Thanks. My roommate just moved out. I'm still trying to figure out what to do with it."

You gave me the tour. It took about thirty seconds. You pointed at the vacant room with the blue walls. You said this is now the dog's room. "Do you want any coffee?"

I'd already managed to down a pot that morning. But, hell yes, I wanted to taste what your coffee tasted like. Because that's already what you were doing to me.

"My neighbor roasts his own beans," you said. "You'll really like this."

This is two people hanging out, talking about nothing in particular, laughing—being criminally casual. Standing on the other side of the counter from you, I felt this real need to have a good time—as almost a requirement of sorts. For now, that was it—to be able to leave knowing that you were pleased and that I was too. And that maybe that was enough—though I now assume there were mountains of other emotions you were quite capable of making me feel. And, I, the same for you.

We took the coffee into the bedroom. You had some tiny paintings on the wall. I wondered if you made them, but didn't ask. I don't know why. I guess, it's because going into the bedroom usually means that two people are about to get a little more vulnerable with each other—and the mind starts racing.

I tried the coffee. You were right.

On the bed together, while scrolling through your Apple TV, you asked what kind of movies I liked. I threw out a few titles, but I also knew there was no time for us to watch some full-blown blockbuster. I had friends expecting me in an hour.

I think it was the moment I wrapped my hand around your arm that we stepped away from ourselves. In slow-mo, our lips drew to that place and, once they did, I couldn't stop kissing your face.

Afterwards, cradled around your body, our hands clenching each other's, you said:

I like the sounds that you make.

I wasn't sure what your day might look like after I left, but I wanted to know how you might go about it.

What I had been so far able to infer was that, compared to mine, you lived a quieter life. As I got shitbombed downtown the night before, you stayed in and had wine with the neighbor who roasts his own coffee beans. Maybe it was better to remove yourself from the noise, from the temptation.

To pay a lot less for a lot more square footage. To focus on other things.

We found ourselves, dressed again, and standing in the kitchen. You pointed at the park out the back window and said that's where you like to take the dog. I asked about the blue tape around the edges of the wall. You explained why the paint job was unfinished, but I didn't understand what you meant.

People were waiting for me. I had to go to them. I asked you, "Does my hair look like I just had sex?" You laughed. "They would have known regardless."

And it's true. Especially after certain times.

After I dialed in the Uber, you walked me down the steps. That's when we fell into it again, against the white wall. I don't know what it was. I said to you, "Why can't I keep my hands off you?"

"Probably for good reason."

You asked if my birthday was off to a good start. But that hardly needed an answer.

"You seem like a chill guy," you said. "We should do this again."

It wasn't a promise by any means, but you still had me nailed against the wall and kissed me once more.

We came up for breath and you explained where the Uber would meet me. I said, "It'll be funny when the driver asks what I've been up to this morning."

I made my way up around the mulch and the grass and the trees to wait in the spot you told me to. The driver arrived and I boarded the Honda. And yes, she asked exactly that question.

To which I laughed and explained nothing, because I wanted to hold it with me.

DEAR PURPLE DRANK

Did you know you were going to do it? Or rather, had you done it before?

Me, I had plans that night. It had become a weekly thing—Mike would pick me up in front of my apartment every Friday around 6:30 pm. On the drive to the volleyball nets, we'd listen to *Forensic Files* and try to predict the reasoning behind this week's crime of passion.

Did she want to get her hands on his life insurance policy? Was he angry about her latest infidelity? Did someone fuck up royally? In most cases, it was the life insurance policy.

You and your boyfriend were in town visiting for—something? You said that you'd spent the morning at a couple of the coffee shops off the Square, that you went to the Terrace to look at the lake, that you still hadn't determined which bar to go to tonight.

Then you asked if I had plans.

I was working from home that day. Only plan was the *Forensic Files*/volleyball excursion. So, once you asked the question that always follows, "Do you have plans?," I said sure.

It was an excruciatingly hot day. Humid, relentless sun, beating the living hell out of the people below. I still should have walked.

But, no, I drove. I drove thinking I knew exactly where you were staying. That I'd easily find a spot on XX Street—no big deal. Turns out, it was a big deal that practically gave me a hot dose of pre-sex anxiety. XX Street was closed due to construction, the sidewalks were bursting with people who'd just gotten out of work, the roads were packed with carloads of people who'd just done the same.

And, man, it was so fucking hot.

So, before we did all the things we did, imagine me in the traffic, windows rolled down, the latest Lana Del Rey booming out of my speakers, dripping in sweat, teeth clenched, muttering curse words—with no end in sight.

I tried to let you know, attempted to text—that I wasn't bailing, that I would find something, just was having trouble at the moment. This is me now telling you why I was so late.

"Fuck it" was the phrase I used as I pulled into the parking garage that charged way too much per hour.

"Fuck it" was also the phrase I used as I parked my car like an absolute jackass.

It felt like crunch time. It felt like any desire I'd held previously had now been sweated out.

I texted you. I was here. I was almost here. Your boyfriend met me at the gate. Tall, blond—he looked like the picture you sent. In the elevator, he said something funny. I don't remember exactly what, but I remember it being funny.

Then, inside the apartment, I was introduced to you. It was a good location the two of you found—nice view of the lake, steps away from the busiest street in the city. Good job.

You were busy futzing with the stereo system. As the music cut in and out, you swore at it, before turning it off altogether. Secretly, I'm glad you did, because whatever you were trying to play was horrible.

Standing at the kitchen counter with me and your boyfriend, you asked if I wanted anything to drink. "Yes," I said. I said, "Yes," very quickly.

You threw open the refrigerator and removed the giant bottle of a brand of vodka I've never heard of. Then you removed a can of that pineapple Red Bull bullshit and a purple Powerade. You asked, "What do you want for your mixer?"

"Pineapple," I told you.

You poured the drinks and we stepped out onto the ratchet excuse for a balcony. I looked down—we were really high up. I told you, "My friends know where I am. If I *fall* off this balcony, they'll know where to find you."

You thought that was funny.

From there, I let you and your boyfriend pretty much carry the conversation. I threw in a couple anecdotes, but mostly, the two of you carried us all to the point of *comfortable*. It seemed like you two really liked each other and were in a place where having someone like me over for a few hours wasn't going to cause any sort of interference.

You told me what you do for a living. I liked that. I told you, "I've known a few of *you* in my day."

Then I made a passive aggressive comment about needing to be somewhere at 6:30. It's amazing how quickly things can escalate after such a comment. The three of us took our drinks and our bodies into the bedroom of the person's condo where you were staying.

We went for two rounds. And you left me temporarily half-blind in one eye. I took your multiple apologies to heart—there's always something that happens to remind us all that we are *human*.

As your boyfriend showered, we made out with each other's faces. Coming up for air, you said, "Wish we could keep doing this, but maybe we'll catch you around this weekend."

At first, I winced (mostly, it was on account of my poor eye.). Then I said, "I'd like that." (I ran into you the next night at the bar. That was as hilarious as it was welcome.).

You rolled away from me to take a sip from your drink. I patted my eye. You rolled back toward me, drink in hand. You slurred, "Open your mouth."

I looked at your red Solo cup. I knew. You weren't really going to...? Yes, you were.

As you took a big gulp from the plastic cup, I opened. You leaned in closer, closer, closer, closer. My lips met yours and you did it—you let go of it inside of me. I swallowed the cold liquid. Then I'm sure I smiled or laughed or something. I gasped, "That's amazing."

Purple Drank, I walked away from the two of you happy as a clam. Eye ablaze, I drove my car back to my apartment, with time to spare to meet Mike. Instead of listening to *Forensic Files*, Mike had the great pleasure of listening to me detail just what the hell had gone down.

I don't even remember your name, Purple Drank. And that mortifies me. But I guess, that's sometimes what happens. Someone steps into your life and does something you'll never forget.

Then, he winds up being known to you only as Purple Drank.

DEAR JET SKI

Some night last fall, when we had nothing better to report to each other, Antonio told me I'd met you. With eyes wide and mouth half-agape, I said, "I talked to *that* guy?"

"I mean, a full-blown conversation."

I suppose I could see myself standing there in the hardly-lit bar, music blasting, fags dancing—how that probably happened. Sipping my drink and going on and on about something that I found funny and that I likely wished equally humored you. Not sure what came of that. Not even sure the context of the conversation. Something about jet skis?

I guess knowing that we'd spoken and maybe even developed a rapport of sorts was the impetus to it.

I scanned the packed birthday room, where I'd found myself directly in front of two or three people that I'd known pretending like they had no idea I was a whole four feet away.

I sipped at my second drink and said something to Mike about how strange certain things are.

He replied with something that wasn't atypical of him in his supportive ways: "You want to go?"

I sucked from my straw and made a mocking face. "I have to finish my drink."

That's when I turned my head to the left, looking past a group of *formers*, to spot you. Right there, your eyes landed to meet mine and a small smile in you formed. Typically, my immediate response to something like this would be to turn or lower my head. My eyes drifted back to Mike. I said nothing of substance and then moved past the timidity to come back up and once more let my eyes find yours.

Someone told me I'd met you. That's all I was resting on.

Your little smile grew wider, as mine did the same. You couldn't even call this acting out of familiarity, because I didn't hold any of that for you. But it didn't keep me from throwing up a little wave and watching as you did the same back.

I want you to know there was comfort in the briefest of attention you gave me.

I slurped down on the drink and muttered something inappropriate at Mike. As I set the drink on the table next to us, I said to him, "Now, we should go."

"Should we say goodbye?" he asked.

"I'm sure we'll see them in no time at all."

Moving closer and closer through the bar to grab my coat, I found and then kept your pretty eyes. I had no agenda. I had nothing to even say. I was simply reacting—taking myself away from past and future, to meet you right there. I put a hand on your arm and said, "Hey, how are you?"

You nodded and said, "Good. I'm good. How are you?"

And because sometimes I'm nervous and a bit of a dork, I repeated my prior sentiment:

"Good. I'm good. How are you?"

I let go of your arm, grabbed my leather coat, and pushed through the door, laughing about something that only I could find some semblance of substance or meaning in.

DEAR STALLION

I'd never made a day of Boxing Day. It only happened because Nate texted me the moment I'd gotten back into town. All he said was, "Bar? It's Boxing Day."

"Is it really?"

For the two days leading up to this, I'd been in a spell—the Holidays had always lent themselves to that. Wake up with the family. Have your coffee. Have your Bloody Mary. And continue until the day ends. This year, the Holidays also lent themselves to me sending a "sexy" photo to two people who I had real affection for, but could hardly have—both for vastly different reasons. Reconnecting, I guess, that was something in itself—some sort of validation that left me feeling alright about whatever. Even if the *whatevers* remained *whatevers* that I *could not have*.

We didn't realize it, but the guys had planned it, us meeting. After I'd finished my Bloody Mary and done a shot of Jameson with Nate, you showed up. I didn't immediately acknowledge that I knew you were in the room, but, I'll admit, I was aware that you were there. And I was patiently waiting for the time when Nate would introduce us.

I said to Nate, "I'd let him drag me around for a few hours."

It was within minutes that we were shaking hands and Nate was telling you that I was a published author, which I laughed about, because that sort of introduction always made me laugh.

What you didn't know yet is the magnitude to which I do not take myself seriously. But you'd find out.

We went to another bar. I saw your friend, the one you came with, I saw him say to you, "So, did I do good?" And then you both looked at me.

I waited for your head to nod. Then your head nodded. We wound up at a round metallic table. I made fun of the brand of beer you were drinking. Then, when you told me as much, I made fun of the fact that you were a Katy Perry fan. You were taken aback when I went over to the jukebox and put on "Only Happy When It Rains." And I liked that you were taken aback.

There were things you had yet to learn, but they were all things that would only come with time.

The guys—all the guys with us—they continued playing into it. Nate talked me up to you. You friend talked you up to me. On that Boxing Day, we might have made sense. To them, we definitely made sense. But that doesn't mean things have to work out sensibly.

We went over to the dart board. At first, I didn't realize how seriously you took it. It became apparent when you appeared pretty pissed about how seriously I did not take it. We were on a team. That one shot I took, when I hit the bullseye and my eyes lit up, I said to you, "Are you proud of me?"

You rolled your eyes and smiled. "Yes, I'm proud of you, Alan." Then your hand fell to my ass and touched it ever so briefly, sending a lightning bolt down my spine. This *could* make sense.

And then you were gone.

And that hurt, I suppose, but it's okay now. Like I said, there were things you had yet to learn about me. Part of me thinks those things could have clarified a lot. They might have surprised you.

That night, I returned to the bar where we had started. I sat down next to this woman who I hit it off with. I started bitching about nothing of significance, while she nodded in agreement. Then she bought me a shot of tequila and I wound up at the jukebox playing "Never Said" by Liz Phair, an unnecessary rage in my eyes. When I sat back down next to her, she told me she was visiting for the weekend, from New York City, and that she was one of Beyoncé's back-up dancers on The Formation Tour.

The randomness of all of that, of that day, how our friends tried to set us up, and what happened in the end—for whatever reason, it's stuck.

ALAN SEMROW

DEAR PETER PAN

All night, the girls and I had been carrying around this blow-up doll with an erect penis. Unoriginally, I'd named him Richard, and we'd had ourselves a banging good time, with this being our final stop.

We are here. This is my best friend's bachelorette party. And, surprise, surprise, we're planning on finishing it off at the gay bar.

Beneath the hazy streetlights, you were standing at door smoking. You said, "Well, hey there," as I approached. Playing coy, I squeezed your arm and went inside. This wasn't necessarily meant to happen, but, tonight, it was bound to—we'd been in sporadic communication for at least a year—flirting, just harmless flirting—and, finally, we were meeting face-to-face.

Out of some gift from the drinking gods, I'd maintained a real cool buzz all night, without going overboard and having to go home before the party ended. We ordered our drinks. You sat with us at our table and explained to the girls your love of Harry Potter.

Theresa, the Bride, she gay-gasped when you said it. She's like, "Oh my God! I'm going to Universal for my honeymoon! We're going to the Harry Potter!"

I can't positively say I was all that interested in what I was hearing, but you were looking cute and you were looking at me like I knew just what you were thinking.

Theresa asked, "So, what do you do?"

You explained and then said, "I also do some acting. I was Peter Pan in a play last year."

Again, Theresa gay-gasped. That's when I rolled my eyes—not at you, but at her. This was typical. And this was our relationship. And we loved each other for it.

I'd smartly reserved two hotel rooms for the night. In the elevator, I explained to Francesca that I would now be needing the room that we had planned to share, to myself and to you, and that she would have to stay with Theresa and Jenna in their room. She understood—I think. Mostly, I think she just liked you and had issues with the word no. We stood there and tried not to watch as she packed her bag in shame like this was some disciplinary action and took herself and the key to the room next door.

And then we fucked like volcanoes.

Laying in each other's arms, you said, "Shall we go have a cigarette?"

So, there we were, walking through that very upscale Hilton, hand-in-hand, like we'd been together all our lives, with dick glitter in our hair and the afterglow rising above. We sat on the bench outside and you said things you probably wouldn't say to just anyone, which I appreciated. We put out our cigarettes and then we were hand-in-hand again.

At three in the morning, we visited the girls. I sat on your lap in their hotel room. They scolded us and we laughed and kissed it off—meaning, we made out in front of them.

In the morning, I woke to the sight of you standing at the window, bare ass naked and looking out at the city, the rising sun. I rubbed my red eyes and said, "What are you doing?

You said, "It's a pretty morning." And so I did. I got up from bed and walked over and looked out naked with you. It was a pretty morning. It really was.

DEAR HOCKEY

Maybe there never was a light switch. Maybe it was some kind of contraption, where there's a string hanging from the ceiling and you have to pull it—like the light in my bathroom in college. I felt around on the outside wall—I felt it with my dick hands. And, wait—inside wall, right there, I had it right there.

And sunshine!

It was bright and you had no decorations on the walls, no little keepsakes. I sat down on the toilet and started to piss. My mind traced back—I couldn't recall the walk to your place, but that hardly mattered right then and there—dazed and confused.

Tinkle. Tinkle. Tinkle.

You kept things tidy. I spotted the electric toothbrush, the Crest toothpaste. I stood from the potty and rolled my underwear back up around my ass.

I turned the light and then I went—that way. No, wait. I went this way. It was this way. I had both hands splayed out in fear I'd run right into something and stub a toe. I patted your bed. Yep, I'd made it.

Good job.

I pulled myself up into the spot where you slept. You rolled over and put a bare arm around me.

"Hi," you whispered.

I giggled. "I made it to the bathroom—thought I was lost. I'd woken from the weirdest dream of my life. And I think I'm still drunk."

"We drank plenty last night," you told me. Then you said, "You're weird. Go to bed."

In the morning, you were charmed—like unable to stop kissing me. We had sex again and then I escaped to the balcony where I smoked a cigarette, standing barefoot.

I snuffed the cigarette out on the ground and placed it in one of the outside corners, hoping that days later, you'd find it and think of what we did.

I plopped myself back on your bed. You said, "We should really do this again."

And I nodded. "I agree. This was fun. And unexpected. And cool."

The night before, I was at the bar with Rachel. And you, because of circumstance mostly, found yourself next to me. I looked at Rachel and then I looked down. I looked at her again and looked back down. I muttered in her ear, "You know, like someone like *that*. That would be nice."

That's when Rachel removed herself from my side to stand on the other side of you. She'd had plenty to drink and whenever she does, she becomes a talk box filled with initiative. She said to you, "Hi."

You said, "Hey there."

She pointed at me. "I'll give you each five whole dollars if you kiss each other at this bar right now."

You looked at me and I smiled. And then we kissed for all the bar to see and, when we were finished, I told you, "You're a good kisser."

That was the start of it, but not our last kiss at the bar. One could say we hit it off.

Back in bed from my cigarette after sex, you ran your hands through my hair, turning me on all over again. I said, "I don't remember walking here last night."

"You were funny."

"How so?"

You sighed. "Well, when we both toppled into the apartment, you sat on the edge of the sink and threw your jacket off and then your shirt and said, 'Come here.' And I did and we started kissing."

I laughed and rolled my eyes. "What a floozy."

"You took my shirt off and we just stripped right there. It was hot. You turned the sink on and ran your hands through the water and then onto your chest and onto mine."

I rolled my eyes again. It would be so like me to pull a Glenn Close.

I stood from the bed and looked at my almost dead phone. You gave me your number. I said, "Where exactly are we?" I told you the name of the street I live on. You said that I was about three blocks from my apartment right now—how convenient.

A day from that night, you texted and asked how my week was going and if I'd want to get drinks sometime. And I responded, "Sure! That'd be great."

This would go on in the same sort of fashion for about two whole weeks, and I wouldn't follow through and you'd eventually give up on me. I want to tell you that, at that moment in time, I was still trying to find my place in our city. I gave up on you as a possibility. Which I shouldn't have. But we all have to be the terror in the picture from time to time—the one who lets somebody down.

Months later, I was walking by that same apartment building—the one three blocks from my apartment. I thought of you and wondered if you still lived there and where you've been. I thought about *possibilities* and the paths we do not take—because it was cool what we did back there. It was cool.

DEAR KISSER

Technically, it was still daylight when Greta and I had gotten to the bar. There were inflatable flamingos all around in the trees, on the pavement of the outdoor patio. Greta bought one for me—the five dollars went to a local AIDS charity. As to be expected, the bar was crowded. It was a big weekend—maybe even bigger than what I'd seen the year before. Watching all the unfamiliar faces floating around, I felt at home. Possibility was a very real thing for me in those moments. I could live here. I could fall in love with someone on this outdoor patio.

This little annual trip, it'd become a bit of a legacy thing for me—an end note to the year I'd had, a gift to myself. Each year, I'd fly out to see a whole other kind of Pride. I'd prepare myself for new experiences. I'd let myself go. I'd adventure and meet new people. Simply put—as I explained to the driver who picked me up from the airport—when I come out here, I allow myself to be the person I don't always feel comfortable being back home. The driver laughed, because he knew what I was trying to say,

At the bar, with all these people that we didn't know, repercussions meant less. Reputations—at least mine—didn't exist. I saw you look. And then I looked. And you looked and I almost caught you.

But, wait, we have to be timid first. We have to let it settle in.

I said something to Greta and then her, in her mild inebriation, said something to you, because I was too nervous. She asked what you were up to this evening and then I introduced myself. You explained that you and your friends were off to another bar soon and that you wouldn't be returning here tonight.

I asked where you were from. I asked you more. I asked if you'd ever return here. You weren't sure.

"Darn," I said. I wanted to get to know you.

So, we kissed right there—you, with your wicked tongue—because we didn't know if we'd ever have that chance again, meeting up from our separate places.

Just wanted to say it was nice.

DEAR TWO WEEKS

In retrospect, the whole course of events runs like a comedy. You, fair fellow, took me away from just about everything for almost exactly two weeks. And what a two weeks it was. We made a stir of things. We knew how to make a scene—the impermanent power couple.

It was St. Patrick's Day. I'd been off dating apps for about two months, which had given me time to meet myself again. And so, I guess, by that point, I was ready for you.

I'm still a little hazy on the impetus. I know I was decked out in green. And I know I'd been eyeing you for some time. But, almost always, you'd met me with disregard, which made me want you more. But that wouldn't be the case on the day we finally introduced ourselves. All I had to do was meet your eyes, smile, and stick my pointer finger up. And there you were, asking about the impermanent tattoo on my neck that read: *Kiss Me, I'm Irish*.

Of course. And I'm hardly Irish.

Running your finger down my neck, you said, "What's that say?"

I let it spill from my mouth. And, after I said it, we owned the room for the night. We leaned up against that bar as your friends' cameras flashed. Here we were. And we knew just where this would go.

You'd be slow to admit that you caught some sort of feelings. I'm writing this to admit that I did. As much as you could really piss me off, I enjoyed our little trip together. And, I think that's why such a scene was caused every time we met up. These were two strong personalities, intermingling with a lot of different people—a lot of your friends who became my friends. Who remain my friends.

Through it all, I was nervous. I felt there was a real opportunity for you to hurt me. And you reassured me of that when you said you were afraid you just might that night at the bar, when we got into a bit of a tiff (and, alas, caused a scene). I believe the last thing I said to you was, "Well, then hurt me." We kissed and I walked home alone.

That didn't stop anything—not yet. There was still the dinner where I got the bloody nose at the table and ran off through the darkened, fancy room, holding my face. And then came back to you, after the massacre had been committed in the bathroom, to only be greeted with a shrug and a slight laugh.

There was still the making out against the light post in broad daylight and being honked at by passersby.

There were still the mornings after. All those cups of coffee I made for you. The dirty car rides. The snarky comments. The laughter. The sexcapades (the mirror, the kitchen counter). The music. There were still all those really genuine friendships that I made as a result of you.

There's nothing in me that wants to point a finger and wrong somebody here. Mostly, I just want to tell you I had fun. I have no idea how often you think about that period of time—the measly two weeks that felt like two months—but I'm happy about it, after all is said and done.

DEAR DESERT GUY

Just like the night before I flew out the year prior, the cat pawed at my feet every hour on the hour, as if to say, "I know I haven't paid you much mind, but tonight that changes."

In the morning, I rolled to my side, acknowledged the hangover, and winced at her, seated beside me all comfortable and innocent.

"You're fucking with me."

I stood from the bed, stumbled into the kitchen—hair shooting into the air—grabbed a mug that read "UW Mom" from the cupboard, and poured the coffee Greta had so graciously prepared.

She's a keeper, Greta. After what happened that afternoon, I kind of wish you'd gotten to meet her. In the meantime, I guess we'll have the picture on the wall.

As had become habit that week, I took my first cup of coffee out onto the balcony, along with a pack of Marlboro Menthols, my phone, and *Dancer from the Dance*. The story of Malone and Sutherland and all the other characters surrounding them, it was starting to affect the way I looked at the people that came into my life, for however brief (sometimes, for whatever reason, it really matters).

Blowing a stream of smoke into the dry summer air, ashing all over myself, the book, and the green carpet below, I pondered how a person might choose to spend their final day.

It'd been a hell of a time—like all the years before, I went into it telling Greta, "This is going to be the gayest week of your life!" Mostly, that went without saying, but she'd been a trooper through it all. She stood by as I made out with men in highly inconspicuous places like the middle of the park in broad daylight, or the entrance of a neon-lit gay bar. She made no fuss about how it took me two hours to "get ready" in her bathroom before going out that one night. She laughed when I got sick on the sidewalk after brunch and far too many grapefruit mimosas.

To her, I was the "Wild Child." To me, she was the "Daddy."

Reading through the crafted, devastating lines of *Dancer from the Dance*, that's when I first caught a hint of *those sounds*. My eyes fell back to the glass sliding door. There stood the cat, paw up, batting at the door. I stuck my tongue out at her and refocused—just to make sure I was hearing this correctly.

Yes, right from under me, it was the neighbors—the delicate (maybe not so delicate?) moaning of man and woman, going at it on a Tuesday morning like their life depended on it. I guess you could say I was humored, but also in the midst of feeling a lot of other things (it was clear they enjoyed each other's company). I closed the book, lit another cigarette, and thumbed my phone on.

And that's when I saw you, faithful stranger.

As the woman climaxed and echoed out into the seemingly vacant neighborhood, I said to you, "Hello."

At first, you had a lot of questions, which I welcomed because it made me feel at ease. On my final day, I could trust you, couldn't I? We'd fall into something and then let the other go back to his life.

You said, "It's a shame you're not from here. It'd be nice to have something regular."

Words, they were, but also words I wasn't so used to. Thank you for being real with me. I agree.

You snuck off from work for me, taking an extended lunch break. I met you in the front lobby. Our eyes met as I closed in on the glass door to the building. To say I was wildly attracted to you would be an understatement. To say I could sense that you were nervous would also be an understatement. First instinct was to grab your tattooed arm and then hold the door.

Hello, Mr. You.

The cat scattered to the bedroom the moment she realized *one* unfamiliar man had now become *two* unfamiliar men. I sat on the bed Greta had set up in the living room—the one she planned to discard after my visit—probably for the better.

You told me about your life before moving here (fellow Midwesterner—many times, you'd visited the city where I lived). You told me about your Pride weekend. I told you about mine. We sat with the space between our conversation. I could have said it, something about the tingle running through my fired-up body—it was hard to play pretend with you.

I can't pinpoint exactly when I knew it was going to happen, but something in me sensed that it was going to happen before it actually did. It might have been when I started digging my hand harder and harder into your bicep, when your breath against my skin began beating heavier and heavier. Or maybe it was that point toward the end when we kept each other's gaze for what felt like an hour, staring into it like a bottomless hole.

This will end and both men will go back to their lives.

We finished together. For me, it was the first time that had ever happened—it was like pushing a button and seeing the light—at the same time. And maybe that's why I found it so hard to let go of you afterwards—even though you really seriously were expected back at work.

After we dressed, you walked around the apartment in small little circles. You told me more about your life outside. You made a comment about the picture of me and Greta on the wall ("You were younger then."). We made no mention about what we'd just experienced, but something in the room had changed. It'd be cliché to call it a *familiarity* that I sensed in you. But it's safe to say my molecules had been altered. The whole year leading up to this, in a way, it was now validated. This was real.

I kissed you at the door. And then I kissed you again. And then, wait, one more. There were no promises made to meet again the next time I found myself in town or to keep in touch after my return home. Perhaps, it was because this all had been exactly perfect, and we both had, with experience, become well-aware of the fact that things typically become less perfect as more time is spent together, as two people become less and less of a mystery to each other.

By not making any promises, we could put insurance on our perfection.

After you left, I drank vodka-waters on the balcony and every once in a while, glanced back just to confirm that the cat was still there, paw up, batting at the glass door.

When Greta returned home, the word I had for her was, "Legendary."

The words she had for me were, "You will never do that in my condo again, you asshole."

Yes, I was a bad boy, but I couldn't feel sorry (not today)—just this time, I couldn't feel sorry. Instead, what I could do was listen as she lectured me during the drive to the airport. Something about you being a stranger. Something else about you being inside of me inside her condo.

Outside the car with the orange suitcase in tow (the one I kept stationed in one exact location of my apartment for months after returning home—just to remind myself), I hugged her goodbye and told her it would never happen again (tehehehe).

The plane wasn't filled to capacity. There was an empty seat between me and an elderly woman. As the sun fell down, I stared out at the pretty mountains, at everything behind them. I was headed back to my life and a lot of parts of me dreaded it. I feared that maybe one day I'd lose what I was feeling in the pit of my stomach for you.

But now—as it's come to be true for me, these things don't ever really need to leave. Sure, they can fade and lose some of the initial sparkle. But they can stay as long as you choose to let them. And, I guess, this serves to say that over many occasions now, I've chosen to let them stay.

As the plane taxied and began to hurry faster, faster, faster down the runway, I listened closely as Harry Styles' "Sign of the Times" blew through my ears, growing into that huge climax with the violent guitars and banging orchestra. It was at take-off, as me and the plane shot into the gorgeous sky, that those two little tears made their way down my face.

DEAR CITY GUY

I picture you walking through the doors of that hotel. You were wearing that black parka and your head had started down, before rising up to make first sight. You could have guessed, but you really didn't know what you were getting yourself into. Just home for a simple weekend, visiting your family for the holiday (What holiday was it even? Thanksgiving?).

Right there, I think we shook hands, didn't we? I don't know why that, of all things, would be the first thing we would do. But we did.

I had warned you that I'd been out *all day*. My friends and I met for brunch. And, me, I guess, I decided to continue it until the time came for what I kept telling everyone around me was "my date." I had a sense of humor about it, because I was well-aware of how the night would probably end. My inhibitions had been lowered and my nerves had dwindled. And it was funny that I thought it such a great idea to meet a guy and try to connect with him, while so obviously being on a different level of intoxication. This is you and me, standing before each other—and now, we're walking to some bar where I'll have another vodka-soda and talk your ear off while you talk off mine.

You'd recently made an unwanted move to a city where you didn't yet feel you belonged. I could relate—it took a while to learn a few lessons here. But now, things like the brunch earlier that day, they served to validate the fact that I had found *my people*. It takes time.

And it can be the most difficult, lonely kind of time.

If only they understood.

You told me that a famous actress lives in your apartment building—that sometimes, you caught her in the elevator with her daughter. Out of fear (or intimidation), you've never introduced yourself. I watched you ramble on about all the fun things you've done and, the whole time, I thought how exciting it must be to live in a city like that. It conjured up a fantasy where, one day, I could live such a reality—a faster, all-consuming kind of life full of even more opportunity. I wanted to immediacy you described.

"Our date" turned into us heading back to the bar where I'd spent the majority of the day. You remained adamant about it and I finally conceded. I told you, "People might have something to say when we come in. Just ignore it."

Thankfully, everyone there who knew what we were up to kept quiet as we zoomed to the back of the room, where I knew we'd be left alone to do our thing and hit it off a little bit more. Every so often, I'd sneak out the back to have a cigarette. And, at one point, you decided it'd be a great idea to buy me a shot of Jameson. We took the shots and I leaned on your shoulder. I said, "Do you know what would be really funny right now?"

"Oh, boy." I told you that you had no idea what you were getting yourself into. "What?"

"It would be really funny if we just started making out in the middle of this half-full bar right now."

As our lips released from each other, I imagine I laughed. I want you to know this wasn't part of some game I played. It was just how I was feeling right there. Because I liked you.

After waving goodbye to the few that remained, we walked hand-in-hand across the street to the hotel. We had sex and then you turned to me and said, "I want to know more."

I threw up my hands and laughed. "Alright. What do you want to know?"

"Facebook said we have a lot of friends in common. A lot of people from where I lived before. I want to know how you know them."

I laughed again and acknowledged that I noticed the same thing, but didn't have the same question for you. I said, "I have a lot of stories. And I've met a lot of people that mean a lot to me. Most of those people that we're both friends with, they're probably strangers. But there are a few of them on there that I do know quite well. But I won't say anything more."

You tried to tickle it out of me, but I wasn't budging. If I'd had one more shot of Jameson that night, I might have. But no. Those names stay with me and I carry them around.

"So," you said. "If you could ask me anything, what would it be?"

"Anything?" You nodded.

I'd been wanting to ask a person it for a long time, just to see, just because I was curious, and I wanted to know if the answer would be similar to my own.

"This weekend, you had just a few days. You were on a tight timeframe." I ran my right pointer finger through your messy sex hair. "So, why did you choose me? You could have tried to woo anyone else in this city. But I'm the one you found. Why is that?"

You placed your bare arm around my hip and puffed air. You whispered, "Well, why not?" And then you followed that with something—it was something very exact and very honest. It wasn't necessarily the response I expected. It wasn't even what I needed to hear. It was just very perfect, I'll tell you that.

We fell to sleep and woke early (too early) in the morning to have sex again. And then it was us, standing at the door, knowing that when you came to visit next, it was very likely we'd purposefully bump back into each other, to revisit, to check-in, to see how two people had changed over the course of a few months, how much more you'd gotten to know your new city—the one you'd drive back to, while I went back to the job that I'd explained I was trying to get out of. But that comment—that thing you said, it kept clutching itself to me.

DEAR RYAN GOSLING LOVER

I saw you. The way I was positioned in my chair, it was in exactly the place it needed to be for you to have a direct view of me, and me of you—straight on. It felt close, yet miles away—you were all the way over there in the orange chair, overlooking the mouthwatering lake.

Over beers on that hot, hot day, Jack was bitching to me in his loud, loud voice about something he found significant. And, I assume, I probably delivered mundane little comments back that made it clear that I felt whatever he was complaining about wouldn't matter in a year—that he should turn down the volume.

As he continued on, I kept glancing at you—right over there—every once in a while, coy. You and I were both shirtless and wearing sunglasses to protect us from maybe the truth resting in our eyes. Your body glistened in the sun, your long-ish blond hair reflected it.

And I got the sense right there. How your Ryan Gosling face kept turning away from your friends who were speaking. While you were not. You looked at me. Jack kept talking. I fell to nodding and laughing to myself that this—that you—were probably something that was happening right now. Whatever I was supposed to be hearing, I no longer did. I looked at you. You looked at me. I looked down and then at Jack as he said all those things, yet nothing at all.

Eventually, it was just: "Bitch, let's just go then if you're not going to listen."

We downed our beers and made a plan to head to another location. I put my shirt on, making a point to ensure that you could see me do so. I lifted the sunglasses from my eyes and onto my head. Jack began walking and I stood, feeling thankful that he chose to walk *that way*.

I saw you. As I passed, I gave that little wink. Just because. The danger in doing that, the thrill of it—I suppose it hit me right where I wanted it to. You smiled.

Goodbye for now.

DEAR LOBSTER BISQUE

Things can end because of how they start—that's what it came down to. We'd been flirting for a couple of weeks—consistent text messages, little snaps back and forth. You revealed to me all the things that I would typically ask on the first interview.

I had two options—that's what you gave me. We could, like, meet for drinks. Or, if you wanted, we could just hang out at your place.

With you—bearded, built, and intellectual—I guess, I wanted to try something a little different—just to see what the results of that were. And so it goes.

Just a few minutes late, you texted: "Apparently, I get every goddamn red light in the city tonight. I'll be there shortly."

When you walked in the room, I'm not going to lie, I leaned just a little to the right and almost fell out of my chair. Social media and all those other things, they'd already let me in on the fact that I was going to have a thing for you. In-person now, it looked like social media was exactly correct.

You were two weeks removed from a surgery. I was in a state of trying to get over something. What a perfect fucking combo. We hugged and sat down. I ordered a second beer while you ordered a cider and a lobster bisque soup.

Mostly, throughout the conversation, what was going on in the back of my head was: *Oh my God, I am wildly attracted to this man*. And: *Don't fuck this up*. Did I, though? Or was it just the fact that I was a little emotionally unavailable and, as a result of the surgery, you were sort of out of commission?

I don't know. And we don't have to talk about it. Because, by this point, you should be at least somewhat aware of how I feel about you.

Outside the bar, a homeless person approached us and asked for money. I let you tell him that we didn't have anything. He walked off. We hugged and I said I had a nice time and we should do this again.

You started your cold walk west, while I started east—back to our own respective places, surrounded by our own little things.

Months later, we ran into each other again—at the bar on a Sunday, where it seemed almost everyone there was in the mood to get a little outside of themselves. You touched my ass, like someone who had been a part of my past—I was happy you did that. And, now, ever since, whatever clumsiness there might have been, it's translated to fondness. And I don't how much more is greater than that.

ALAN SEMROW

DEAR GREAT WHITE BUFFALO

It had been at least a year since we'd last seen each other—you met me at a time when I was younger and vacant, vulnerable. And emotionally unavailable. I want you to know that I was here for it the night we reunited—out of happenstance, out of my persistence to maybe make it up to you in some way.

You must remember the night we met my boss and coworker for dinner at the Mexican restaurant. I told you it was a nice place and you said you promised not to wear your hoodie and sweatpants. It was small things like that that made me thankful to have that moment in time with you. After hanging with them (and after you stepped away to the bathroom and they'd given you a ten-star approval rating), you drove my car back to my apartment because I'd had too many margaritas. We only realized it on the freeway, when I turned the music down and identified the weird rumbling noise—you were driving in the wrong gear. We burst out laughing. "If that just killed my new car, you owe me another."

You said that wouldn't be the case.

That night, we had sex on my Serta air mattress (you had a similar one back at your apartment). While you were inside of me you kept saying that thing that makes me feel something to this day ("You feel so good."). Anyone could say those simple words, but you gave them the meaning.

I thought about you all that time after we ended—after that night when we stood out in the courtyard sharing what I presumed to be our last cigarette. Before I walked off, we kissed on the mouth.

When I saw that you were back in town, I said what I did to you because Monica told me I'd regret it if I didn't. That night, I got ready at her place. We shared some wine and I told her why meeting you again after all this time was so significant to me. On my way out, I almost hugged her goodbye, before reminding myself that, although things were all well and good in the world right now, she was still my coworker, I'd see her the next day at the office, and she hated hugs.

Exile in Guyville played on the way to your hotel. I passed spots that I used to pass while driving to you—little restaurants, gas stations, resorts. I looked forward to those drives—that night you took me for pizza, the night we caught the drag show, the night we spent at your friends'—dog-sitting, doing bad things to each other, watching your weird Netflix shows, listening to all that music you liked so much— the stuff I still have on my iPod. Whenever one of those songs comes on, it pulls me back.

Parts of me think we could have had it all, but timing is a real bitch.

Upon my arrival, you texted to say you were on your way down to the lobby. I stood in front of the gold elevator doors and watched the numbers above *ding, ding, ding*. My stomach was lit. And then the final *ding*. And the doors. You had that tiny smirk on, the one that used to make me wonder if I could actually trust that you weren't going to hurt me (like the one who came before you), but now made me swoon.

You hugged me. You looked and wore the same cologne—for that, I was grateful.

Things were going well today.

We'd kept in very sporadic contact since the last time—the little pokes over the course of that year, the pokes that served to not even check in and see how the other was doing. Mostly, I think it all just served to say that we still floated through each other's minds, all this time and, now, all these miles away from each other. You bought the book and sent me a picture of it in your hands the day it arrived in your mailbox—a brief chat ensued. But I wanted to tell you more.

Tonight, you were in town for a work conference. You'd fly back tomorrow night.

Walking through the lobby, you asked if I still smoked cigarettes. I said, yes, sadly. You told me some story about how you'd managed to quit for a few months but were back on it. Then we went outside to share one. This was weird, wasn't it? That something in me felt it so incredibly necessary to revisit things—just for the night, just to see, just to set things right—maybe? Or maybe there's no question at all as to why I felt it such a great idea. Maybe it's one of the smarter things I've done.

Your rental for the week was a mini-van. As we approached it on that chilled night, I laughed. You used to drive me around in that tiny little silver car of yours. Now, we sat a fucking Dodge Caravan like soccer mommies. You drove from your hotel, back to that bar you used to frequent—the one where we met your friends and I got to see a side of you that I hadn't yet. We left them to go find trouble as a duo.

We walked in and Ed and Dan ran over. They introduced themselves to me, though we'd met a few times before—if they only knew what we'd done while dog-sitting at their place that weekend.

Mike bought us a shot of Fireball and you told them all the things that I'd been wanting to ask you, but didn't know how to. How did you like your new city? Your new dog? Your new job? Your new life? Did you miss your old life? Your old friends? Your family?

You stood from your stool to put that song on the jukebox. I bopped my head and mouthed the words and asked you about the latest record by that band you like so much.

It's poppier, isn't it? But not really a bad thing.

We stepped out to the enclosed patio. You were starting to get a little tipsy and I think I was, too. It was cute when you got like that—giggly, talkative, full of random anecdotes. We lit cigarettes and you started telling me that you had this idea for a book, that you'd always wanted to write one, but didn't know how. I leaned in closer and said, "Tell me more." And you did. I wish I still recalled the details. All I recall is it being a story—one big metaphor for what was happening in our world right now. As you went on and on and on, I think my face, it grew redder and redder and redder, my eyes, shinier and shiner and shiner. I said, "That's the hottest thing I've ever heard," similar to that thing you once told me when you saw my book collection for the first time ("That's the hottest thing I've ever seen.").

I grabbed your face and we made out in that enclosed patio.

You didn't care what anyone thought of you. You judged no one. You befriended people you liked, of all ages and sizes—with no pretense. You were weird and you were real. And you held my hand that one night at the theater during that special showing of *Casino*—you held my hand for all three hours of it.

You looked down at your feet and back at me and said, "So, how late are you planning on staying out tonight? Or, are you going to drive home? Or, to your friend's? Or...?"

This was our moment.

"Well," I told you. "I brought a change of clothes tonight. It's in my backpack."

The little grin on your face told me that you knew exactly what I meant and that you were absolutely okay with that—with us maybe doing something we shouldn't do.

Ed and Dan bid us farewell. In that empty bar, they said, "Behave, boys." We plopped back into the Caravan. You turned the engine, but before you backed out, I touched your hand and said, "Wait." And I bent over to kiss you. "God, I missed this."

In the elevator up to the hotel, you said, "I still have that book you lent me."

It was the Amy Hempel collection. I was well-aware. For a bit after that night in the courtyard, I resented you for getting it. Eventually, I came to terms with the fact that there was no reason to be angry at all. We'd had our time and it's important we did.

As the elevator doors opened, I said, "I know you have the book. I wanted you to keep it. You also have the *Sophie's Choice* DVD." I touched your shoulder and stepped out to our floor.

In the room, we discussed Don DeLillo. You said you didn't like *White Noise*. I told you that it'd been a while since I'd revisited that one. I cracked a beer and we made eye contact that seemed to keep at a glacial pace.

Your pink, wet skin against mine, it pulled me back to the way it had always been (hot as fuck). It pulled me back to the first night, when we drank that bottle of wine and discussed politics and religion and watched *American Horror Story*—when it just ended up making sense, when the conversation was so good, when both of us agreed to infer that this would continue.

The weekend after our first night, I drove up north to my dad's cottage. While everyone was out hunting, I sat on the pier overlooking the twinkling, calm river, reading the novel you'd lent me and drinking a vodka-water. Things were good, things were where they needed to be. And I couldn't even try to get you out of my mind. That day, I wrote a song about what I was going through.

I woke wrapped in your naked body. My alarm rang at an obscene hour that I think you had hard feelings about. I rolled out of the bed to shower. All your stuff laid out on the counter, perfectly placed—it was all the same stuff you used to use. Same toothpaste. Same hair gel.

I dressed and then stood before your sleeping body. I slid onto the bed and straddled you as your eyes slowly opened. You winced. "It's early." I nodded and said, "I have to go. But I don't want you to be a stranger. I want you to have a good rest of your time in town. And I want you to have a good flight."

I kissed you goodbye and left. It was too early for anyone to be out and about in the lobby to witness the beaming yet flustered fucking look on my face as I made my way through the hotel. I entered my car and "Glory" by Liz Phair played. It was right then when I was able to truly understand those words—because what she was saying was exactly what I was experiencing in real-time.

You are shining some glory on me.

As I drove off, my eyes glazed over. I knew there was no guarantee I'd ever see you again, that we'd ever find ourselves in such a circumstance where it would make absolute sense to repeat this.

But also, I think that's okay, because we still went back and got to do what we got to do—even if it was the last time, it was the perfect ending.

DEAR AFTERNOONER

When Greta told me you'd be joining us, my eyes grew wide and I said, "Another gay?"

She let out a guttural laugh and said, "Sometimes, there's no need to even wonder what your reaction might be."

You worked with her at the nonprofit downtown. She said you were a really nice guy and that I should just take it slow. She didn't really know your story—if you were seeing anyone or not. But I was on vacation, so fast-forward to us, in the park during the Pride event. We'd gotten to the end of the vendor booths, around the Capitol. Greta had purchased The Gayme—the reason why, I don't know. I bought a few t-shirts. We all had plenty of beers. And then you and I snuck away to make out on the lawn—in broad daylight.

Just take it slow, she said.

Maybe I could say I was going through something at the time. Maybe I could say I was on the verge of dismissing all those *somethings*. But mostly, you were sweet. So, you gave me your number. And I said, "I'm here for three more days. And we should probably have sex."

You laughed and nodded and said, "That sounds like a great plan."

Greta was something else. Two mornings later, as we were sitting on the balcony drinking morning coffee, I told her that I wanted to hang out with you. She said, "Where does he live?"

I read the address you'd texted me the night before.

"Shit. That's not close at all. It'll be a $30 Uber one-way. At least."

"Eh," I said, waving a hand in the air. "I'm on vacation. I'm here to spend money."

"No, Alan. I'll drive you there. I have some errands run at the Target. I'll drop you off and then you can just call me when you're ready."

I don't know how I got so lucky to have her in my life. But that's what we did. Harry Styles' "Sign of the Times" played on the radio on the drive over. I said to her, "I really dig this song. It speaks to me."

She nodded. "I could see that."

The conversation paused and then I started up in a fit of laughter. "You're literally driving me to my dick appointment right now. This is golden and I'll never forget it."

She brushed it off. "I'm happy to." Which made it all the more hilarious to me.

I texted you as we pulled up. I exited the Honda and, there you were, standing at the glass door. You waved at Greta. Walking towards you, I turned to watch as she waved back. I almost flew back into hysterics right then and there when she shouted out the window, "Have fun, boys!"

You let me into the house that you shared with some elusive individuals who obviously smoked a lot of pot—from the plethora of artful bongs scattered throughout. You told me you owned none of this, only what was in your bedroom, where we found ourselves lying on the bed. You asked me about my book, which had come out a little less than a year before. Then you explained the novel you were working on. It sounded like you put a lot of thought into it—that you took it seriously. And I liked that about you.

You turned to me. "Do we like have sex now?"

"Yeah," I nodded. "I think this is the part where we have sex."

You turned up the music and kissed me. Then you rimmed me. You used a condom that you'd gotten from one of the vendors at the festival. While I was wrapping it onto you, I thought how funny it is that everything seems to come full circle.

It was hot and sweaty and open. And, when we were done, we just laid together—for a period of time that seemed endless. Finally, I opened my eyes and saw yours right there. "Greta might be done shopping now," I whispered.

"Okay." We both starting dressing, in the quiet of the afterglow, until finally: "Will I ever see you again?"

"Yeah," I said. "You will, because I come back here every year. And I'll call you when I do."

I've learned leaving things is sometimes better than letting them drag out, and discovering that the other person isn't who you thought he was. I'd have to fly home in a few days. There was nothing we could do to hold ourselves together for an entire year—no matter how connected we felt in that moment. But I wondered what it would be like to. Maybe you were someone that I was supposed to find out more about—to spend time with. To really investigate. That afternoon, you made me feel like maybe that was the case. You were years younger than me. And I was attracted to that. You held this innocence—like, just starting out in your career and wondering where the world might take you. I missed those pieces of myself, when things were less black and white. And a lot seemed much more promising. Sure, I have all the intentions in the world of seeing you when I'm in town next. We can fall into all of this—once again—

and, at the closing of it, tell each other, "Until next time. Until next time, my friend."

DEAR NAPKIN

That's all it took. One flimsy, white napkin. Filling out my tab, I must have had *True Romance* on the mind. You know, how Patricia Arquette writes that thing before the big shoot-out.

You're so cool.

That's not what I wrote to you. But I gave you similar sentiments. I wanted you to know that I thought you were cute. That you should have my number. And we should explore—at one point or another.

I was steadying out the screeching door when Tommy said to you, "Go get him." And then you were running out behind me. I looked to you and your eyes ablaze. You said, "That was one of the sweetest things anyone's ever done."

I laughed at the ridiculousness of the notion—the reason I was here wasn't to be *sweet*. Not yet. I waved my hand through the air. "I was just being honest. Thought maybe we could get a drink sometime."

"How about now?"

"I'm heading to Stella's. You should join. They're all pretty chill."

She met us at the door with eyes wide. "Well, hello."

"Stellaaaaaaaa, this is my new boyfriend." You wrapped your arm around my torso, squeezed real tight, and we laughed at ourselves.

Right there, our bodies were changing, becoming more and more familiar with the other.

We were starting to think it could happen.

Upstairs, we poured the wine and you regaled everyone with your stories—the places you'd been, the people you'd met, the campaign you worked on. You were a traveler. You had a lot of opinions. You wanted me to know.

I thought, how have I never seen this person in my life? And, also, how will I feel about this person in the morning? When the party is over and we all have to return to work.

By this point, summer was coming to an end, but tonight, we were blessed with warmth and just enough of a steady wind. I stood on the balcony with you—for just a moment alone. You held my hand and we looked out at the glowing moon and the lake below it. We own this. We own all of this.

"Some place," you said.

"I know some amazing people. Some amazing people with really nice views."

We kissed against the metal railing. Took a second. And then kissed again.

The entire walk to my place, you held my hand and you said stuff that I'd forget. In between all the things that men in lust do, I think we got about three hours of sleep—I was meant to remember that.

After the next morning passed, we tried for more. *We tried*—the drinks over pizza on Wednesday, the sex session that followed. And then I failed you. I can't write the words as to exactly why. But I did. Which doesn't mean I don't think back to how we came together. Or the silly napkin.

DEAR ALMOST STRANGER

It all happened so fast. I met you at the door. All you had to say was, "What's up?"

You followed the five steps down to my studio apartment. I swung open the door. We walked in. And, almost immediately, you dropped your pants to the floor and threw off your shirt and that navy-blue baseball hat. By that point, I felt like I'd seen it all, but, still, I was shocked by the forwardness. How little you looked around the room to maybe, even by accident, gather some tidbits about me and the life I lived. How little you gave a shit. I'd had time to blink maybe once, twice.

You said, "Massage?"

So, this is how it's going to be.

I trailed your lead and removed my clothes. For my birthday, Stella and Sarah had given me a quality bottle of lube, hemorrhoid cream, and massage oil. I just want to make it clear that one of the three had been done as a joke. I grabbed the massage oil from the desk drawer.

By this point, you were face down on the bed. I saddled up and straddled the small of your back. It wasn't yet clear who was in charge, but I had a sense.

While making the arrangements, I told you I was in heat—that this always happens when the seasons change. You'd essentially said the same, but with less words—you told me a massage turned you on soooo much. So, this was us fulfilling a need. Trembling against your wet back, it was my skin, your skin, and oil, slipping and sliding all over. A swirling conduction, fixing for the volcanic eruption.

It's true it had been some time since I'd last given a massage. My mind traces back to one night, the autumn before, with somebody I liked. From what I heard, you enjoyed whatever half-assed bullshit I was doing to you. I leaned into your ear so that you could hear my breath grow heavier and heavier, and so that I could hear yours do the same. I drew myself back and gnawed my hands into you. Shoulders, upper back, lower back, down to the ass, where I'd linger—and then back up again. Repeat.

Digging into you, my body became increasingly aware of exactly what we were generating. Anticipation, desire, need, fire—I wouldn't break from quivering through the entire lead-up—two people bound to translate into some kind of shining skyrocket.

With teeth nibbling your ear and hands on your hips, I waited for you to turn over to face and kiss me in the impersonal way that you did—as if you saw meeting mouths as just something people who have sex do—a necessity of sorts. It was clear you had no intention of knowing me. And maybe that's what made it all the more powerful—*just this time*. We could ram into each other and never have to face any sort of aftermath, any kind of residual anything—because this was fucking for the sake of fucking. It was human. And it was natural. And it was carnal. Nothing mattered—we removed ourselves from our worlds, our histories, and prepared for take-off.

You flipped me over, smacked my ass, took me from behind, and set me ablaze, before spinning me on my back and, with each thrust, plunging in harder. Right there, facing you, I hated you as much as I loved what you were doing. Manly, rough, raging. When, finally, I grabbed the reigns and landed myself on top of you—that's when the fire in your eyes and the sound coming out of your mouth told me you would probably reach your limit. Seeing as much put me in a place to reach mine.

I let go on your sweaty, convulsing stomach. And then, you—your eyes rolled in the back of your head and you yelped once, twice, again.

With your cock in me, I folded onto you and waited until the panting stopped. We kissed once more—for the last time—because I felt like that made a lot of sense, considering. You rose from the bed and I watched your ass as you pulled your jeans over. "Big plans for the rest of the day?" I asked.

Placing that navy-blue baseball cap on your head, you huffed and said, "After what we just did, I'll probably need a nap."

Your lack of—what was it?—caused me to not inquire further. But we'd still done something. And, now, it was time for us to leave it as almost-strangers.

You said, "I hope that was as hot for you as it was for me."

I nodded in agreement, in my sudden pride. "That was really awesome."

"We should do it again sometime," you said. And I've heard it before.

At the door, I hugged you ever so slightly and kissed your cheek. Then you were gone. That was all. I was left alone. And you were, too—destined to gain no further knowledge, destined to never do it the same way again, destined to move the bed back from the other side of the room where it had ended after the frantic, precise, perfect movements of our soaked bodies together.

DEAR PHOTOGRAPHER

I'm still not convinced of the importance of it. But it happened. And I still have what you gave me.

We met maybe a month or two prior at a party. Over the course of the months that preceded, I'd gotten to know a lot of the people who were in attendance—friends and more-than-friends. Things like this made me nervous, so I stuck by you and our mutual friend, Darren. Mostly, we just watched—and maybe drank to compensate for whatever we felt the need to compensate for.

The weeks that followed, we kept in sporadic communication. And you started it. It was nothing to write home to Mommy about, but I liked the attention and the thought of *prospects*.

What I now realize is that I should have dove in during *those times*—when you were providing an opening for me to hop through. It's too bad, but timing—

What you should know is the amount of attraction I have towards you and your sunny face. What you should know is that I'd like for you to get to know me. But I now know that might never happen. And it pains me that there are parts of me that some men will never know.

I'm not sure what was going through my mind that afternoon. My friend, Kaitlin, she was in the process of moving somewhere new.

This would stand as our final outing together. We met Stella, Sarah, and Mike. From there, we landed ourselves on multiple patios for a little Sunday Funday—something I'd really come to enjoy and gotten very good at. The sun was hot and the drinks were strong.

And, apparently, I was in the mood to make my move on you—after all this time.

Our conversation started innocently. I said a few things, asked about your career, told you what I was doing. Enough talk of the leather bar led to me calling you "Daddy Bear," which you absolutely were not. Though I think you understood the irony, you detested the nickname. I had a few laughs, a few more sips of my drink. My friends continued their conversation.

But my focus was on you.

I told you we should meet up sometime. I told you that I was attracted to you. I sent you a picture.

And then, yes, sitting there with some of my favorite people in the world, the sun beating down on us, growing tipsier and tipsier with each drink—you sent your very carefully taken photo.

You, standing there, bare and raw and aroused.

My mouth flew open. I muttered, "Oh my God." My friends asked what was going on. I wasn't in a place to answer. It wet me. It threw me out of my element. And almost out of my chair.

Cancelling the chase and pouncing at the intended outcome produces varying results. Maybe we'd gone too hard. Maybe the mystery was removed. Maybe I'd given you a version of myself that you didn't think I had in me—ultimately, turning you off. For whatever reason, that was the last day we communicated. It's sad when I think of it—the fireworks we could have been, what those fireworks could have led to. That gorgeous picture made me want to explore—that's all.

DEAR CARD DEALER

That first night escalated quickly—when the majority of us flew just a touch out of our elements, only to allow experience to take the wheel until we passed out into oblivion. We landed in the morning and reconvened to revel in all the things that had been said and done.

Kenneth backed into a dumpster with his brand-new car.

But, Alan, you're a bottom.

The entire house essentially became a hotbox.

Tears streamed down our faces—it had been so long since I'd laughed so hard. I felt happy and at ease.

A few weeks later, you met me and Stella for brunch. That day, I don't know if I was bound and determined to stay out with you for twelve hours and learn more before impressing myself upon you, but I kept whatever I was selling (for a while, at least) and you stayed there with me as morning turned to night. I kept a steady buzz. You hardly drank anything at all.

You taught me the card game. You gave me a hard time. When I snuck away for a cigarette, you ran out in the winter cold in just a t-shirt. Your eyes ablaze with restrained worry, you said, "I thought you left." I blew out a stream of blue smoke, laughed at you, and shrugged. "I'm only smoking."

That day with you, as people that I knew and loved passed in and out of where we were, I think I mostly remained afraid of going back to myself—back to my apartment, where it was quiet and I became the person that no one else really saw—a tamer version, reflective. What I would have done was open a book or my laptop and write whatever words I felt compelled to. I'd look around at the things I owned, the little keepsakes that I've kept to remind me (I still have those cards).

We hit it off and, truthfully, we really didn't need to stay at that bar for so long. We could have left at any time and had our way with each other. But, no, this was different. We were taking our time. And, I think by the end of it, our situations had changed—or at least the way we looked at them and each other. Questioning, maybe. Unsure of what move to make next. Fond of each other.

It says something that you stayed with me—that we made friends with that couple from Utah. They were so nice. And you were, too. The kissing and the petting that resulted was the cherry. It reminded me of simpler times, when the rush that resulted in climax wasn't necessary. When it was just pretty cool to be around each other, when patience mattered.

DEAR ATLANTA GUY

Hair on your chest, beneath
The yellow shirt
I want to see you in full
You smile when you talk
When I do, too
You make me wet
For you.

I fantasize taking it all
To the moon and back
We'll rest with this
The things we said
Do you feel it yet?

Look into each other's eyes
And linger
Patio full of people
And stop
Do you feel it yet?

DEAR STEAK

With you, it came down to the small things. The sunny afternoon you met me on that crowded patio for a beer. We kept it going for some time into the night. And you were relentless in your pursuit. We wound up in your car. We wound up back at my place. You held me close against your wet, naked body and we fell to sleep. I whispered that I had to be up really early. Which was true.

At the time, I was still new to the city and it turned out being a busy summer. I didn't know anyone, but there was no stopping me in making sure that changed. One of the first *ones* ended up being you, which didn't mean I was in any place to give you the attention that I wish I'd given you upfront. Distance—a trip to Vegas, a trip to Philly—it made things manifest, it made me see clearly what was standing right in front of me. But, by that point, I think you might have already been gone?

Yes, the little things. Every morning, I pass the restaurant we walked to on the second date. There, I drank wine and ate lamb. I think you had chicken, in some sort of carrot puree. You told me about the time you had spent out West, that you intended to go back soon. I imagined a young you, traipsing along those dirty streets, looking for *something*.

That night, when we were having sex, you turned brilliant. You said:

Get up. I want to take you against your door.

So, that's what we did. The walls of my apartment building, paper thin. It was the middle of the week and we were taking things to that level, *ooh-ing* and *ahh-ing*, sweating and panting, against the wood door, our sounds echoing out into the hallway. Anyone who might have walked by, they would have heard. Anyone who had been on the same floor even, they would have heard.

It's the little things that I hold onto. At the time, I was desperately naïve and had a lot to learn. As I see it now, if I had known those things when I met you, we would have worked a little more cleanly.

Every time, at your place, we went through those certain motions. Neither of us could ever decide on dinner. We'd debate and debate. We'd watch good movies, we'd watch terrible movies. On the couch, you'd hold me like someone you've known for a very long time. You'd hold me the same way someone that I used to know used to hold me. Then, we'd fall into fucking at all angles, in secret little hideaways of your house. The ring of the doorbell. The barking of the dog. Me, running to the hallway. You, wrapping Badger a blanket around your nakedness to accept the order.

I'd let the dog out. You'd fix the broken garage door. I'd yell your name when the glass of the porch door unlatched and fell on me, making that loud boom. You'd say, "You're amazing," as my body trembled with the heat of yours, before coming.

I'd tell you, "I like you." And then in the morning, I'd shave and get ready for work and leave a little black sock tucked away in the corner of your room, just knowing that the next time I saw you, you'd present it to me freshly washed.

I can still evoke what your house smelled like. That wax scent you burned. You kept it all so tidy.

But, it's true, we had to start having conversations. I came over one night, really late, after you'd gotten done with a long work shift. You poured me a glass of wine and looked in my eyes and said, "I just wanted to check in and see where you were at with things."

I guess, we spent some time coming back to each other after that, but there was mounting pressure on both of us to make up our minds, to feel something, to really feel the need to need something. We kept at it, through summer, into fall, into winter—where we officially ended whatever we had started. Now, I can see that all of it made me nervous—the attempts to meet each other where we were at.

On a Friday night, I kicked your ass at bowling and you weren't happy about it. In that room full of people, we listed things about ourselves that the other might not know or realize, doing whatever we could to connect on *that* level. I learned about your family. You learned my favorite book, my favorite song—that I use my computer mouse upside down. In the car, we sang along to "Philadelphia Freedom." We were dead and gone, and it would take me a long time to reconcile with the fact.

With you, it came down to the small things. I passed out cold on your couch one night and woke in the morning to you making me a cup of coffee and putting on PBS programming. You, almost getting towed out of that spot that you were always so adamant about parking in, but that you really shouldn't have parked in. That one night, I got so drunk I lost my cool at the gay bar.

I've passed a point of looking at my mistakes with you. Now, all those things, they only sit in there like little shiny stars that I allow to glow every so often. We got real with each other and I think that's saying something. And if we could do it all again, you probably know my answer. I've seen you since—it's me walking up to say hello. We hug. I touch your face. And I say, "You've grown it out." Butterflies flutter through my stomach—the thought of your breath against my skin, of the time we spent together.

DEAR CLEAN-CUT

There wasn't really any reason we needed to let each other go that easy. You'd travelled a good 50 miles to "run errands" and meet me for lunch at a place I'd never really cared for, but a place where I'd been on little "interviews" a time or two before.

You were good at conversation. I can tell why you've been so successful in the line of work you're in. Breathing confidence, exuding charm. And, I'll admit, sitting across from you, the thought crossed my mind that I wanted to be your one and only—at least for a time. It crossed my mind that, on the weekends, I could drive to you and we could have our way—rising in the mornings with you cooking eggs and sausage. I'd take the dog out. We'd go to the mall. We'd have sex on top of the dryer. Little thoughts. Innocent. Not reflective, per se. Just thoughts, dreams.

We started the inevitable walk to the car. You said, "Now, don't be getting yourself into too much trouble today."

"I won't." But there were things about my life you were yet to understand. Little did you know, it'd be quite the game day. I'd lose the keys to my apartment building in the pitch black of night. In the hopes of finding an alternative to entering my apartment, I'd hop the tall iron railings to my porch, smashing the side of my face against the pavement—bloodied and bruised and panting.

I made a comment to you about how your car was parked next to its twin. Matching black SUVs. You pointed at the poinsettias in the back that you'd purchased earlier. I nodded in agreement to the frivolous things that we do in life.

In the middle of one of the busier streets, we stopped and hugged. I said a few more words. "We should really do this again." And I hoped for your reassurance that we would.

One last hug. Our eyes lingered there just a second or two. We had time. And then you moved in to meet me with that super clean kiss that sent me right to the top of the moon and back. It was either the perfect end note or a signal for what's to come (*this is either the first or the last time*). My mind started racing, wandering.

I don't know what I said next. But I know I said something.

All that followed was you waving me off and opening your car door. You yelled, "I'll text you later!" I stepped away from the middle of one of the busier streets, smiled, and started the walk to meet Mike and Sarah at the sports bar.

DEAR FIRE LIGHTER

A woman and man and their young children walked by as I leaned into the shiny wall across from your door. I did my best to not make it awkward—*I'm just waiting for a friend*. A housekeeper passed. I grinned. She gave me nothing in return.

For a Saturday, it was a bit early for this sort of mischief. But I was attracted to you and had been on a roll lately, trying to find and figure out something very specific.

You cracked the door and whispered, "Alan." The use of my name alone was just about enough to convey to me that you gave a flying fuck about the fact that I'm also a person with real feelings. You were older and, it was clear, had experience in the game.

I whispered back, "Hey. I've been out here forever. People are giving me looks."

"I'm naked," you said.

I laughed and slipped through the crack in the door.

I didn't look down right away to see what I was playing with here. Instead, I looked into your brown eyes and smiled. Then my eyes moved to the candle in the corner of the room. What was that scent? Was it campfire? And was it really necessary to be burning candles in hotel rooms? Was it for mood, or did you just really like candles? I should have asked. I've always wondered.

The day before, you said you'd been at the bar I frequent. I asked what time. Turns out that I must have just missed you. Which is good for us, because, if we had met there, I'm not sure this would have happened quite how it did. It's all about timing and location. I've learned that.

You kissed me on the mouth and wrapped your built arms around my body, which is what I wanted most—to be held. As my breathing grew heavier and my heart pumped faster, we began pulling off bits of clothing. The white t-shirt, my yellow shorts, the rings, the Pride bracelet, the socks—everything. You felt your way across my torso and chest. And then you said, "Come here."

We fell onto the bleached, white bedding. And I thought how nice it is to just be naked with a man—in all your horny rage—and make out. To take the time to feel around—your parts moving along his warmth. Wanting it—but waiting for it. That makes it all the more volcanic—the end result, the time in between now and the end result.

The bathroom door opened. That's when your husband found himself on the other side of me. He kissed me on the mouth. Then he directed my head down to your cock.

I gave you lip service. Then I gave him lip service as you gave me another kind of service.

It was you who dominated the whole scene and it seemed your husband liked it that way. The two of you were very in love, had been together for quite some time, and understood each other on a deep, deep level. That's what I appreciated most. How that *deep level* translated into something that cared about my needs as well. Cared that I wanted to walk away from this feeling something similar to what you wanted to feel. By this point, I'd long given up on the notion of having sex just for the sake of having sex. It was more than that. I wanted experience.

As you slammed into me and I breathed into your skin, your husband stood behind and touched your body. He touched you. Then he swung around to touch me. There was no forcing anything. There was no clumsiness or tension. It just *was* and, out of some sort of unspoken agreement, the three of us had the liberty to do whatever the hell we wanted.

And I wanted exactly what we were doing.

While your husband took the reigns, I looked over to the corner of the room. It was you, seated next to a glowing candle, watching us, touching yourself. Right then, your husband removed himself from me—like he sensed it or something. You said, "Alan." And, with just one finger, you lured me—crawling over across the room to you on that chair. The carpet below, it burned and marked up my knees as I gave you something and your husband, under me, gave me something back.

It was hot, you know? It was. But, beyond that, you both showed me more.

After we were done, your husband ran off to shower. I began putting on my clothes, piece by piece by piece. The white t-shirt, the yellow shorts, rings, Pride bracelet, socks. And you just talked. You told me your plans for the day. That you really liked being back in town. You asked me about my relationships. You asked about my friendships. I told you, "I'm going on a lunch boat today with my family." I laughed. "And by family, I mean the people that I *only call* Dad and Mom and Crazy Aunt. They've taken me in. I'm the Son. It's deep. And it's one of the greatest things to ever happen to me."

You smiled like you meant it. You said, "Well, that sounds awfully nice. I'm glad you found yourself a little *family* here, Alan."

And I was glad to have had the afternoon that we did. It made my weekend. And as far as I could tell from the little sweet nothing message I got from you later, I suppose it did the same for you.

DEAR SUNSHINE STATE GUY

During the day, I was instructed to fulfill a real responsibility, to sit in a room full of peers and learn *things*. Come night, I found a whole city waiting for me to go leave a mark, which is why I wound up in front of you at that empty bar.

All day, you'd been at some soccer function (all the locals were talking about it)—day-drinking with your beers and your good friend, Ted? The bartender, Kyle, who I'd befriended the night before, he introduced me to the two of you. We made conversation, and once Ted(?) left, I asked your name again. And then you almost called your Uber. But I whispered in your ear, "We should like make out right now." Still not sure what compels me sometimes.

So, we did. No one was there to pay us any mind—besides Kyle who I figured had seen it all.

You said, "I want to take you home with me."

I shook my head. "I have places to be tomorrow morning. I *really* need to be at those places."

"I have a plan."

You left the bar about fifteen minutes before me. I boarded the Honda CR-V and the driver, she had some gorgeous hair and smelled like Goldie Hawn. She said, "How's your night going?"

What a question.

"You know," I told her, nodding my head. "It's been a hell of a year."

My mind traced back to what we'd just done in that bathroom. I thought back to how into it we were—that this isn't something I'd get away with in my home-city.

"Has it? Well, that's damn good then. Keep it up."

My lips pursed and my eyes narrowed. "I mean, I think I've lived a full life. Like, if I…"

"Bitch." In one quick movement, she nodded her head down and then back up, the beautiful black hair splaying through the air. "You have not lived a full life. How fuckin' old are you?"

I told her.

"Okay, honey. No. You got a whole lot of years to go. You have not *lived a full life*."

And she was right. But it made me laugh, in the context of everything. She dropped me in front of the hotel. I walked through the marble lobby, past all these rich people, dressed to the nines, who'd either worked really hard or done the absolute bare minimum and gotten by through pure intimidation—or by just being really good talkers.

I probably didn't belong here.

In my room, I turned on the lights, removed my shirt and shorts, and stood before the bathroom mirror. I looked in. I thought, damn, this is good lighting. And then I looked at myself just a little more.

DEAR DADDY

Over several weeks, we'd shared the innocuous and impersonal details of what, I'm going to go as far to say, were much more complicated and personal lives. We both came from something before we came here. And, behind all of that, was experience and joy and hurt. And all those other things.

Daddy, you bet I was interested. And I knew it would only be a matter of time. We had mutual friends. You showed your interest. I finally made the move—because it all can flash by before it's gone.

That day, you shared the things that really, really turned you on, and, as you did so, I fed into those little tidbits of knowledge—out of intrigue and arousal.

Fuck yes. I want to get wild with you.

Take me away from my hell.

At that job that I couldn't possibly imagine myself working for even one more month, your messages lit a giant fire that served to say that there was no way in hell I could come out of our afternoon together feeling disappointed. This sort of sureness, pre-encounter, was rare. Often, nerves played a bigger role. But you gave me reassurance, Daddy. And kudos to you for that.

We met at my front door. You stood shorter than I thought you were. And wore different clothes than I thought you might. You had this, like, boyish charm—or, I don't know what I'd call it (it hardly matters). Although there was very little age difference between us, you held an innocence that differed from me. Maybe that innocence contributed to why you went about your sex the way you did. You weren't jaded. You led a pretty chill existence and you floated through life. I wish I had more of that. You turned me on. And I wanted to meet your rage.

Ultimately, it all flew together in that popper-scented haze, body-to-body, hair, a lot of aggressive words flying back and forth. Words that served a very particular purpose.

Once you said, "Oh, that's a good boy," you had me exactly where I (and you) wanted me to be.

I was so game for you, Daddy. I was so game to be Son.

Every slap on the ass. Every bite on the lip. Every tug. Every thrust—it gave me just as much pain as it did everything else. The fire was something that, in the shower afterwards, we could only laugh about.

Yes, that just happened. Pinch me.

We parted and you went off to your volleyball game, while I went off to softball. Out in the field—right field, where nobody hits the ball—the only thing I could do was think about how I wanted to sit with you again. Because, really, there was no reason for us not to continue doing what we had that afternoon. It's just hard to say these things, I guess. I've been trying to get better at it. Efforts and results have varied. But I want you to know that I sat with (and felt) what we'd done that afternoon for many, many days. I still think about it. I think about—*things*.

DEAR BLONDIE

It was cute the way that you said the things you did. A blunt sense of humor that put me in my place:

Come over tonight and clean my apartment for me. I know you'd be good for something.

For me, it all came off with a wink and you're lucky it did—with most, it might not. I was in town for a concert. A two-day-only special with my best friend, Jack, who, by the time we first made written contact, had rolled his eyes at me about a million times—the night before, the noise complaint call from the front desk came in while I was belting "Love on the Brain" into a remote control. He looked at me with wide eyes and told me to shut the fuck up already.

Jack means a lot to me, you should know. He gets me in ways no one else does.

You were at work during those initial pokes we gave each other. From my place, seated on that hotel bed, far too early (I had already pissed Jack off with the jackhammer sounds of the espresso machine), it seemed like you hadn't really had much work to do at all. More recently, I'd learned what that felt like. How we return to our devices. When all else fails. I was happy to occupy you and your snark.

You said, "I'll hide you away, because I know that's what you want."

And I laughed and traipsed across the room with espresso and phone in hand. I slid the shade to let in a small stream of morning light. I looked out at the street below as Jack snored away. Even this early, even in this bitter cold, the city held this undying energy that I envied and wanted to be a part of.

It's true that you weirdly attracted me and that I had all the intentions in the world of meeting you face-to-face—just to see—but communication dwindles as the drinks are poured, as the money is spent. Apparently, you'd shown up at the bar where we'd been. By that point, I was passed out in the hotel—asleep, with what I imagine to be a half-grin, reveling in how lucky I felt to be able to do things like this every so often—little weekend trips away from reality.

But we did find each other on the little social medias. And I want to say, every time a little something from you pops up, I'm reminded of what kind of fire we could light. I'm reminded of how I'll do my best to seek you out the next time I return to your city—for some concert, or just because.

I imagine what your voice might actually sound like (you said you're from the South). I imagine what that hair might feel like, my fingers running through it. I imagine a lot of things a lot of the time. And, I'll say this—you had me laughing. And I'd like to have you make me laugh more.

DEAR VOCAB

The next morning, you had me spinning. I walked from your place to mine to the bar, where I met Jack for brunch. I stepped into the room and, anybody there could have sensed it—I was floating. A glowing face, a gleaming smile, something that gave off the impression of, "I could die today and all would be okay."

Skipping up to the table, Jack's first response to me, "Bitch. Contain yourself."

I took a deep breath and my eyes rolled into the back of my head. "I'm going to be honest. I think I'm floating on the periphery of something."

We'd gotten around to spending two nights in a row together. I held your hand. We fucked all night, all morning, between sleeps, between me straddling your warm, pink body, and looking over to the wall and then back to you and then back to the wall. "I LOVE that picture."

It was on the floor, leaning, like you had no intention of hanging it again. But, the strong political message, I guess, it stuck with me—with all that was happening in our world.

You said, "Oh, yeah?"

"Yeah," I told you. "I really LOVE that."

Running a spare hand up my right arm and breathing into my ear, you said, "Well, you should have it then. I'm planning on getting rid of it, anyways. On getting rid of a lot of this stuff I have no use for." You said, "I *want* you to have it."

I didn't take it, because I think it would have been a little much for me to step into broad daylight, looking like I'd had sex all through the night before—hair shooting, eyes red and wild, carrying such a picture the six or so blocks back to my apartment on the busiest street in the city.

The night before, we made out at the entrance to the bar, right in front of the bouncer. Then we walked in to meet our friends, like nothing had happened.

It's a deep attraction I have for you—you, who, every time we've run into each other since, gives me that look like, I could throw you down right now and you know we'd come out of it changed. And it's a fondness—me walking around your sunlit apartment some morning, picking little pieces of clothing up, scattered throughout, shouting innocuous jokes at you, and looking out at your amazing view and the orange sky and saying, "It's a beautiful day. It's a really beautiful day." I meant that. I wasn't selling anything. I stood out on your balcony, bare feet against the cold concrete, smoking a cigarette. None of this was mine, but in some ways, it felt like it was today. In some way, maybe.

Back in bed, unclothed again with my arm wrapped around your body, your friend, Amanda, entered the apartment to unbag groceries for you—I still don't understand why. You said her name. She looked in at us, the lovers, and then left. We fell into a fit of laughter and had sex again. When you were inside of me, you muttered, "You're so hot." Nothing in me desired to stop doing what we were. You wanted to explore every part of me—and I wanted to do the same to you, to eat you up in our moments together.

After spending time on each other for the umpteenth time, I looked back to the picture on the wall. You told me about your life before this city—about your upbringing, your schooling, about the guy that had you for all those years. After dousing my mouth with your spearminty mouthwash and applying your hair wax in an attempt to make myself at least semi-presentable to the people I would pass on the walk home, I kissed you four times at the door. I remember that. Exactly four.

You left my body in pain for three whole days. But it was the best kind of pain. The pain that reminded me. After returning home from brunch with Jack, I locked the door and collapsed onto the wood floor. I was outside of myself. I took a deep breath.

That all just happened.

I ran a bath. I think I sent you a picture, the scent of the bath bomb simmering me down. Spring was turning into summer and things were going well. In a way, I felt validated—for whatever reason. And I planned on always going back to floating on the periphery and looking into your eyes as you took me away. It made me question things. Like, what will this mean in the end? What could we have been? I can tell you with assurance—all good things.

DEAR TRAVELER

I liked how quick you were in your responses. It was Friday and I was seated at my desk, gazing blankly into a computer screen, having zero intention of doing anything significant. I'd gotten myself into a situation where ANYTHING else in the world seemed better than having to come to this office one more day to have my soul—the soul that had been so nourished at my last gig—sucked from me.

Your prompt responses were needed. They took me out of that world.

You told me that you'd seen me at the bar the night before. Typically, I'd react to something like this wondering what kind of shit you might have seen me getting myself into. But, last night, I had behaved and gone home early.

You explained what you did for work and what it was you in town for. I was equal parts turned on and envious. I was sure you felt fulfilled. I was sure you'd worked hard to get to where you were at.

You talked travel and, once we hit the point in the conversation where two people are sure they are probably into each other, you said:

I'd like to steal you away and run to South America.

"When?" I asked.

"I like to do these things spontaneously."

I welcomed that. And I welcomed meeting later that night, when you were done working. It was getting late—you texted as I was walking home from the bar, to which I did a 180 and headed right back to where I'd started. Because we don't always have these opportunities.

It was Rebecca's birthday, which meant she'd be tanked by the time we finally crossed paths. It also meant that I'd be a few margaritas in. In the darkness of that bar, I asked you if you needed anything to drink. You said, "I can't drink on the road." And then I understood that you'd either wind up judging me or finding yourself amused.

I told you, "I think I've already had one too many."

Rebecca, she stumbled down the middle of the room, hand on her mouth, looking just like she was about to throw it all over the floor. I said to you, "That's my friend, Rebecca."

You said, "You should go help her."

And you were so right. I want to thank you for being right.

That's how I wound up in the women's room holding her hair back as she muttered things at me that I could only respond to with nods of the head. I called her an Uber. And then it was just you and me. We played darts and bonded. Outside the bar, you said, "Where do we go from here?"

That started the walk back to the hotel. I think I grabbed your hand, not knowing how you'd react. We had sex. And then in the morning, waking burrowed in your warm naked body, we had more sex. You told me that I needed to not be loud. I let you cover my mouth. The way we went at it, it was like two people who'd been enthralled by each other for a long time. It was personal and it was close.

Our last kiss, it was the two of us, standing by the window. I grabbed your face with both hands. And then that was it. I left you and walked home, allowing what we had just done to move through me, reflecting on where this might sit in the context of my year, of my life.

I texted you after your return home. "So, is that trip to South America still happening?"

"Yes," you said. "It'll be spontaneous."

"I'll anxiously wait for that day."

DEAR GUY FROM COLLEGE

It would be negligent for me to say that you started it. But, I will tell you this: you came at exactly the right time. It was a period in my life—that certain phase when a boy turns into a speck of a man and starts realizing all the things—the important things—that he'd kept pushed down and in denial about through the lead-up to this exact point. What you gave wasn't anything of particular substance. What I mean by that is it wouldn't have looked suspicious or thought-provoking to anyone watching. To you, it probably meant next to nothing. You'd simply found a new friend to talk to in a couple of English classes—as you completed your final semester. To me, it was a lot more—and I've kept pretty quiet about it ever since. But parts of me wish you could see me now.

Things had started to turn around. I was making friends. I was distancing myself from assholes. I was getting good grades and taking pride in my coursework. I was writing a lot. But I was also shutting down. I didn't know how to *really talk* to anybody anymore, because what I wanted to talk about—what I really needed to say—I didn't know how to say it. I didn't know how to face myself at the end of the day. I didn't know how to reconcile with the fact that you, the one who asked me all those inquiring questions and showed interest at a time when I wasn't sure I wanted questions or interest from anyone—you were part of what ripped it all right out of me.

I'd enter class with earbuds in—sweatpants on, probably some very unfashionable pair of shoes (camouflage moccasins served as my way of "making a statement."). And you'd turn your head right then and there as I positioned myself in the chair exactly behind you. "Well, hey."

You were so fucking happy and I wanted to learn everything in the world about you. I also wanted to kiss you after our night class, against the brick wall outside that building. For you to fuck me in your car.

I thought about it. I thought about it a lot. Every mornings in the dorm shower. What it might feel like if you were my first time and could take all the energy I'd bundled up and pushed down for twenty years right out of me. I wanted to see what you looked like without clothes on. I wanted to feel your milky skin against mine. I wanted your scruffy face gliding against my smooth one. To turn red with you.

You made me see that I desired to be more than the *best friend*. It was true—I longed to do all the things that my friends had been doing all those years. I wanted to have sex. I wanted to kiss. I wanted to fall in love. I wanted to have my heart broken so badly. You kept me going. You kept me wondering.

It was the type of attention you'd give me that made it very clear you were interested in the way that only a straight person could be. You made comments: "I saw you walking with your guitar today." It's laughable now, but *that* meant something to me—that's how desperate I was for connection. You gave me something to run with, to think about—to see you as the model of the type of man that I could see myself spending the rest of my days with. Short. Modest. Creatively inclined. Dark brown hair.

A month after you graduated, it came time for me to give myself a break, to come to terms with the fact that I'd been a *good person* all my life and all those things that I'd been saying to myself, repeating to myself, beating myself over the head with—those things were all a means of tucking the truth away. I told the first person, my best friend. And then I came out loudly.

In a way, I suppose you did start it. After my announcement, I went on a six-month long creative renaissance. I read hundreds of books. I wrote books. And songs (one about you) and poems and screenplays and everything in between. I even painted—collages, acrylics. What I was in the process of doing was learning how I wanted the rest of my life to look like—or at least, what it *could* look like. I lived vicariously through the lives of characters—gay characters. And then I stepped out of it ready for whatever might be thrown my way. To be my own character in my own story.

It wasn't picture perfect. It wasn't what I thought it was going to be. But it led up to a time where it became absolutely essential for me to break out of the suburbs and those small towns and cities where I'd spent my life and go somewhere where I could find my second family. Where I could become a part of a community. Where I could come of age and experience the shit out of my life and my relationships.

There's a distinct line between now and the period (approximately twenty-four years) that I'd been without this city—without all these people that I've met and had my moments in time with. The line is there because, before, I hadn't really been *living*—just writing this takes me back to the fact. But, now, I can safely tell you I am. So, thank you.

DEAR LAWNMOWER

We lasted two days. On day one, I came to you in the early afternoon. You introduced me to your sister, the sister that was living with you (is still living with you) in your basement, the sister you referred to as "really mean." We only spent hours on your bed, talking, watching some show that I decided I liked only because you did. We fucked around with the Alexa. She played us hip-hop.

By mid-day, I was starting to think it could happen—it's just like me to do that.

And so it goes, with the spaces between the conversations—what do we say now? How can I get through to this person? How will he see (and understand) the traits about myself that I cherish, but am, for whatever reason, hiding? We lay there and, eventually, we kissed.

You said, "Let's go to the garage." And I thought, that sounds like a GREAT idea.

You lit your pipe and handed it to me. I took a small hit and explained that you can't let me have too much—that if I did, you'd see the exact version of myself that I didn't want you to see.

I sipped from a cider bearing the same name as you. We laughed about the fact. You took another hit and you took me back.

In you, I found a certain naivete—an unrelenting dorkiness that I could get behind. You were aware of your qualities and you owned them. You'd achieved things in your life that you were proud of. And now, at a certain age, you lived your own life in this really nice house that, it was clear, you had worked painstakingly to put together—that was still in the process of receiving its final touches. You weren't sure about the paint in the kitchen. You weren't sure about the knobs in the bathroom.

As afternoon turned to night, we sat on those metal chairs and you puffed on your pipe. Every so often, in between your hits, I'd take one. And, with each one, I think the two of us would reveal something new. Peeling the onion, I suppose.

You told me those personal tidbits. You introduced me to what was happening in your life. And, in no time, the onion was peeled down to the core and you sat before me, vulnerable. I wanted to tell you something, too. Something that would assure you that things would get better. That everyone would get along again, but I couldn't. I didn't have anything, in my current reality, that matched it. Instead, I just listened. And attempted to apologize for others' behaviors without coming off as patronizing.

What you did was tell me about the things that people don't see in a person upon first-meet. And, for that, I'm grateful and want to thank you. You were high as a kite and maybe even drifting from the purpose of my being with you that day. But you were also offering something that not everyone gets.

Your eyes, red and hazy, they met mine. You took another hit and sucked in. In that little half-voice, you said, "Come here."

I knew what you were doing and I was pleased with it. We leaned into each other's faces and I opened my mouth. You blew the sweet smoke inside of me. I inhaled. And I exhaled.

"No one's ever done that to me before," I said, half-laughing. "But I always wanted someone to."

You grabbed my hand and said, "Come with me."

You took me through the backdoor, out onto the grass. It was the time of year where summer was starting to turn into fall, so in the dark of evening, our feet were cold, just like the air. You began walking in circles. You said, "Doesn't this feel amazing?"

And it did—the grass did feel nice. You told me that what most people do is cut too much of their grass off when mowing. Instead, what you should really do is try leaving it a couple inches longer, to cut less. It's better for the health of the lawn.

Above us, the moon, it was almost full (or was it?) and, below us, I guess we had some exceptionally healthy grass. I felt like a tiny kid again, being introduced to the little things—it served to remind me that sometimes, the focus needn't be on the large.

We went inside and had sex.

Cleaning off with you in the walk-in shower, I said I was hungry. You said we should go for a drive. That was how we wound up at the custard stand in the dark of night. In the car, you stuck a spoon into your barely-eaten bowl of cold chocolatey goo and raised it to my mouth. You said, "This was a great idea."

I licked the ice cream from the spoon.

It's moments like this that can make a person nervous. Everything is good, things are new, but you don't know where it will go—if it'll last. I didn't know what you were thinking or whether you'd made a judgment call. All I knew was that this was nice and exactly what I needed that day, that time of year—after the year that I had just had, all the things that I had put myself through. It's something to be nervous about, but it's also something to rejoice in. Stop this moment in time right now, I thought. Just pinch me before we have to go back to being *something else*.

I see you since we've faded. The night you were at the bar, drunker than me. I looked at you with hunger when you came to say hello. I gave you *that look*. You said, "What?" "Nothing," I told you. I gave you the look again. You said, "Why are you giving me that look?" We made out right there, next to my friend, Mike. It took me back. It always takes me back, seeing you. So, I guess, it's clear there's a point to a lot of it.

DEAR NEIGHBOR

Just the day before, you'd moved into the building—when we must have spotted each other near the front entrance. You messaged me later, "Thanks for your help. We only had that huge mattress to carry up the staircase."

"Did you see me?" I asked.

"Well, yeah. I was the one in the staircase with the huge mattress."

"Oh, my bad. Sometimes, I don't pay attention."

That was a lie.

Around 2 pm the next day, after finishing my poor excuse for a lunch, you were barging through the door of my apartment. You'd requested that I keep it unlocked. You also requested that I be laying on my bed, wearing next to nothing—only a pair of short blue shorts. So, I did as told. You swung open the door and said that thing you always say so casually:

Hey, what's up?

You met me on the bed where we wasted no time digging into each other—and, I mean, *really digging*. It was that one thing you did with your hands—where you grabbed both sides of me, in that one place—that made me feel like I might shoot through the goddamn ceiling. And your grin told me that you loved every minute of it—of the rage in my eyes, of the crude movements of my body against yours. I huffed, you huffed. I growled, you scratched. I said your name and you said mine.

You spent the weeks that followed taunting me and I fed into all of it, because you'd left me lit and wanting more—wanting that fire every day for as long as we could handle. I thought about it. And I mean, I really thought about it—the skyrocket we became.

That one afternoon, I was seated at my desk, working from home, and there above through the window, it was the familiar shape of your body, dressed in your black running garb, doing your little pre-run stretches, right against the wrought iron railings of my porch. *Down. Up. Down. Up. Down. Up.*

You knew what you were doing and you knew that I knew what you were doing. Reminding me, though I'd hardly forgotten. You texted later:

Did you see me earlier?

You little deviant. You made me want to know the whole story—how you spent your weekends, how you made money, the music you listened to, what a day in your life might actually be like.

How one encounter can make a person wonder these things continues to baffle me. But that's sort of the point as to why we do the things we do to each other. We're seeking answers and resolution.

Before barging through my door once again, you continued with your little messages and comments and side glances and smiles in the hallway that said to me, I know how bad you want it, but if I make you wait just a little longer, we might make the entire building topple over the next time.

In my mind, that's almost exactly what happened. I'd been out for a bit with Jack and a couple of other friends and returned home and then you returned home and then we returned to where we left off. But before doing so, before finding me on my bed in the exact placement you requested, I heard the outside door swing open and then close. I heard footsteps, but not many. You know I'd kept the blinds wincing just enough so that you could be validated in your perversity, which in turn, allowed the same for me.

Once again, I had followed instructions. You re-entered the building, I heard your feet clomping down the staircase, and then you pushed open the door to my unlocked apartment.

Before flying onto me, you said it:

Hey, what's up? Like some sort of bro that might ask to shoot hoops later.

That night, something happened to us over the course of a little less than an hour—it was whole and complete and I was dying for more. We ended with me straddling your soaked body, looking into your eyes, and asking a few pressing questions, which you were reticent to give answers to. But I learned things. You were a scholar. You weren't from here. You had a membership at the same gym as me.

I grabbed your hands and put them against mine, like a stupid move you might see in a Katherine Heigl romantic comedy. To the beat of "Patty Cake," I clapped our hands together and then fell on top of you in laughter. This was what you did to me—you made me wild and you took me far away from whatever the fuck was happening in my life and whatever the fuck had happened before. I wanted to sit with it. I wanted to take a bath in it and think about exactly all of the things we had just done.

So, thank you. And thank you for telling me that one thing I'll never forget:

My passion is your pleasure.

Somewhere along the way, the fire fizzled, because, to at least some extent, it always does. But before all that, I loved the night when you returned home from wherever and passed me smoking on my porch.

You said, "Hey." Just, *Hey*, this time. I looked up and smiled wide and said *Hey* back. It was simple and casual and all I needed from you—there was comfort in the certain level of familiarity we had formed. The notion that we could actually understand each other, if we decided it made sense to take the time to. You were wearing this blue coat that you'd later tell me was given to you by your host family in Spain. You should know how true it is that I could hardly contain myself and wanted so much more.

And that day at the gym. When both of us ran around it, knowing that we'd quite recently known certain parts of each other but pretending we didn't (ultimately, we *both* knew what we were doing). You were wearing earplugs and listening to music, so you weren't able to hear what I whispered as I walked past to pick up those dumbbells from the shelf. You'll never know what I said. For that, I'm proud.

I continue to pass you—maybe even once a week or so (*Hey, what's up?*). And, I'll tell you, I get a kick out of still winking at you in the hallway and patting your shoulder at the bar—it takes me back to what you did to me in just a few tiny moments. Reminding me that I'm no angel and that's okay.

DEAR WEEKEND LOVE

We had that shiny little weekend. Just two days where we lusted after each other and made empty promises that we'd have to return to and face, once the week started up again and we had to be distanced for a while.

There isn't anything about the two of us that's remotely similar—apart from liking dicks in our mouths, I suppose. I mean, I can only imagine the look on my face when you asked:

Who's Sheryl Crow?

Or when you said:

Do you wanna go shoot some rounds sometime?

It's fine. And there's no denying that we did have *something* during our time together. In fact, we couldn't keep our hands off each other. You presented a lot of things that weren't my norm—that wouldn't generally attract me. And maybe that was the attractiveness of you.

You did your own thing. And I appreciated that.

A few weeks ago, I revealed that you might have a place in this collection. And, so it goes, you do—you who had me up against the brick wall outside the bar late at night—kissing and licking my ear. You, who, after revealing that you really probably do have a place in this collection, I kissed once more—for old time's sake.

Our little weekend, it was calming. Which was nice, because a lot didn't seem so calm in my world at that time. So, thank you. This one's for you.

DEAR MAPLE LEAF

Nearing 9 pm, it started with *knock, knock, knock*. You'd told me you needed to be in bed by 10. And I convinced you that we'd make it 10:30—at the latest—and that it'll all be worth it.

I walked into the hotel behind this woman, probably around my age. She gave me a slight look, as if maybe I'd just followed her all the way out here—to this Hilton on a simple, cold Tuesday night. I think it only took one stiff glance back for her to realize I was a total homo and totally harmless.

She got off at the second floor and I shot to the fourth and, *knock, knock, knock*.

None of this was absolutely necessary. It was a week night. I'd had a long weekend. I was tired and everything else was going pretty alright. But you seemed nice—like a gentle kind of nice. And I thought you were cute—like totally and utterly my type. And we also had limited time—you were only here for work and, seeing as where it was you were visiting from, there was a high chance you'd never return to my city—and I'd never see you again.

Knock, knock, knock.

It took you a while, which panicked me.

And then I heard that gravelly, whiskey-soaked voice. "Yeah?"

My stomach dropped and I grabbed the phone from my pocket. Was it really happening? Had you totally made me believe that you were someone you weren't? Was this my first catfish?

I messaged you. "What number, again?"

You told me. I looked at the door. Yes, 419. I googled the location of the hotel.

"Yeah?" the gravelly voice said. "You need something?"

Oh fuck.

"Uh… Uh… I think… I think this is the wrong door. I'm so sorry."

Google told me I was currently at exactly the incorrect Hilton on the west side. That there were two Hiltons and I'd driven to the wrong one.

Fuck. I muttered a big quiet *Fuck* and barreled back down the hallway to the elevator. I messaged you, "I am so stupid. I'm at the wrong hotel. I will be there in 15 minutes."

The elevator hit the second floor. The woman from before entered. She looked up. I laughed. She laughed. "Hello, again," I said. "I'm at the wrong hotel. And maybe I deserve this."

On the dark, dark drive to you, I want you to be aware of the sense of remorse and duress I was under. I didn't let the music play. I didn't eat from the bag of raspberry gummies. I didn't smoke a cigarette. I focused and cursed the devil, then I cursed myself—all while coming to terms with the fact that this was so very typical of me, that this was so very clearly something I would have done—in a mad dash to find you that evening. And I knew I'd have a good laugh about it later.

Alas, second chances. I tried again. *Knock, knock, knock.* You opened the door and we fell into a giggle fit. I told you about the gravelly voice, I told you that this is something I would do—I was the guy who was bound to make an embarrassment of himself, before presenting the person he wanted you to see.

You had the Olympics on. You explained that your country had been doing really well. And I joked that America had been doing well the *entire time* (I honestly had no idea if that was true and I also made that clear). You threw in a few jabs about my country, our broadcasters, the music played to celebrate the occasion. And then I asked you where Alanis Morrissette and Sarah McLachlan were. It was random and it was funny and it was honest and it was sweet. After making it known that sometimes I am a fool (because it's better to be foolish than to take yourself too seriously), maybe I didn't feel the need to hide much at all—to give you some half-assed version of me? And I got the sense that authenticity was pretty innate in you—you didn't hide. You weren't from here.

I stayed cognizant of time, because I knew you were staying cognizant of it, too. So, eventually, of course, we fell into it. We kissed a lot. And then we really fell into it, before coming back to earth and laying with each other on the bed, catching our breaths. You said, "Why are you shaking?"

"I guess it just happens sometimes," I replied.

Mostly, I was about to fall off the bed and was holding onto you—because I wanted to and also, because of how our bodies were tangled together, I needed a grip. I didn't want to tell you how amazingly uncomfortable I was in my current position, because I didn't want to move from where we were right there in that moment.

I do wish I'd gotten to see you once more before you flew back—to see a little more of that innocent snark. To maybe see the things that made you tick. But did anything? I got the sense that nothing did, that you lived your life optimistically, wishing people well, no matter their treatment of you. It's admirable, really. And so was how gentle and understanding you were to me that night.

DEAR PRETZELS

You met me before I got here. I traveled two hours down just to find you. At that point, I was desperate for adventure. Something and someone, far away from where I was. I needed to connect, because I felt like I didn't have much else going for me.

That night, we went to the bar that I now frequent quite often (too often). We had two drinks. By the end of those, I said to you, "I think they make their drinks strong here."

You laughed. Now, I know why. We ran home together in the pouring rain. We held hands and had endless sex on the carpet—my knees hurt for days. We danced around your studio apartment to the sounds of those music videos. We watched movies and I wound up having to explain why it was so significant that Elisabeth Shue fucked Nic Cage right before he died at the end of *Leaving Las Vegas*.

What you don't know is the time we spent together during that little "adventure" helped make it clear that this is the city where I belong—at least for now. You know, I had a nice time and I wanted to see more of this place I'd never really known. Like many of *us,* I'd come from a small town that could never be *home*. In my younger years, I was mistreated for being *me*. I lived in worlds I never belonged. Now, it was time to release myself and all the decisions I'd made since coming out. I was missing things. That was evident. There was a whole world out there. A lot of new personalities.

Opportunity was real. My night with you put me in this new place. A place I'd move to just a few short months later.

I was determined. This is my commitment and my homo-manifesto.

I saw you that first weekend, after the move. I made it awkward, because I hadn't yet understood that you *can* still be friends with the lovers you've had. It's a choice and I needed an education.

We wound up together again, months apart. It's true that you were with me when I fell into a brick building and scraped my knee and hurt my elbow. In the morning, I woke to a text message from you. And, later that day, I cried into Jack's arms asking him what was wrong with me.

I needed an education.

The next time, I was in a clear, more at-ease place—it's amazing what time and persistence can do. I told you it wasn't going to happen. And then it did, hand-in-fucking-hand again. We made out outside the holiday party, the back of my head pressed against the brick wall. We wound up back at your place. Old familiar. We walked in. "What the fuck happened in here?"

"I didn't have a chance to clean!"

It was a clarifying moment, just like a lot of my moments with you. I don't know why. But thank you for helping me make that important decision—to fly away from all the things I'd known. I still have the chocolates you slipped into the pocket of my leather coat.

DEAR PERSON

By now, you can't deny the fondness I have for you. It's the little re-visitations that pull me back to that very day, when I was living in a period of innocence—unaware of possibility, naïve to what it can do to you. It's these little re-visitations, always messy and always brutal and always so heavenly, that take a notch right out of me and replace it with something else.

We met crossing the street one day. I was standing at the stoplight, surrounded by strangers (I'd just moved to the city two weeks prior and knew almost no one). The signal turned to the little walk-man. I started before the crowd of people. And there you were, right there, wearing the baby blue hoodie, with your friend, James, by your side. You said, "Do you know where the parade is?"

I smiled and bit my lower lip. "Well, I'm new here. But, I assume it's where all the rainbow flags are."

That was the day it started. The day we wound up spending together. On account of my being oblivious to common themes not to touch on with a prospective *someone*, I was completely open with you. I told you what had happened before the move, how a part of me had been killed, and I had been left in a yearlong tailspin—alone. I told you how I had to move past the tailspin and this was the only way I figured to do it. I told you a lot of things, and I want you to know all of them were my truth.

The parade ended. We went to some bars. At the volleyball nets, I was your cheerleader. You played the cornhole game with new friends, while James sucked a guy off in the bathroom. Each time you threw a bag in the hole, I clapped my hands and yelled your name—simple and timeless, it rolled off my tongue. You looked my way, shook your head, and grinned. As each moment passed between us, it became clearer and clearer to me how badly I wanted the most of you.

During the drag show, you handed some dollars to the queen performing. I leaned over to James and said, "I would marry him." I was half-joking and he may or may not have passed that information onto you, but what I do know, is that we could have ended it parked in front of my apartment—one o'clock in the morning, it was now Monday. By this time, I had learned the things that I had wanted to learn about you—the things that validated what I was feeling. You had a past, you were someone I could trust, you liked me. I turned to you. And I kissed you and I let go. We could have left it right there and said, it's done, that was perfect, and we'll remember this. But I waited for your reaction to see if it reflected mine. You said, "Woof! I thought you were going to sorely disappoint me. You are damn hard to read."

I explained that sometimes it takes time to weigh the situation. You didn't live here. We could part in the morning and never speak—that's not what I wanted with you and all the shiny sparks flying around.

The sounds we made. The spot you came. How you toppled over onto my numb body and embraced me tight. I whispered, "I could run a mile right now." It was always the little things—you, standing from the bed, putting your dark blue underwear back on, walking to the bathroom, with one ass cheek prominently hanging out. I wanted to giggle. And I probably did.

The next morning, before you headed back on the long road home, we made out in front of my open window. You lifted me in the air. Once I was grounded, you grabbed my junk and slapped my ass.

I told you that I'd had a really, really nice time—that I wanted to keep in touch. And so, all that summer, we did ("Happy one-week anniversary," you said. "Happy one-month anniversary," you said.)—at a time when I was beginning to bloom into the guy I wanted to be, between the trips to Las Vegas and Philadelphia—before we lost each other (imagine me in the bathroom at work, standing there with the door locked, looking in the mirror extra-long to let my red eyes glaze over and return to normal).

You had given me the moniker "kiddo." We had sent sexy photos. You had told me you wished you were cuddling me. We had tried to make plans. I was leaning into the fire. And you were unsure.

In winter, I found you again. It was after something you said ("It excites me that you'll still have me.")—a weekend trip to your city with no real expectations, apart from the fact that I wanted and needed to see you and reconnect—check back in.

Though there were spaces between our conversations—returning back to something that hadn't really *been* in months, resuming where two people (now changed) had left off—I could still look at you the same. For a while there, *you* were the hard one to read.

But ultimately, you gave me the entire weekend and you should know just how much that means to me still. We danced at those clubs. You introduced me to your friends. We ordered a giant pizza and Diet Coke. We had a lot of sex. In the morning, I woke to the cat between us in bed and the scratches down my back. You made me pancakes and extra-caffeinated coffee.

At the mall, I bought you the whoopie pie. You took a bite and said, "You wanna try?"

You smushed the pie into my face. And there we were, back to where we'd left off. And you were giving me mountains of joy. We boarded the rollercoaster and screamed like little girls, next to the children who sat unamused. We spread out on the couch that night, watching that show that has come to have a special place for me, the new candle I'd helped you pick out burning behind us.

In the morning, we ate brunch with James—the morning I was supposed to leave and head back to my tiny life. In the car that I was so glad to be in once again, you pointed at all the places you used live—or used to frequent—the path where you ran. I think that's when the city was burned into me. This *could* be home. I *could* make a life for myself here. I fantasized. I still do.

Before my departure, you ran around the bedroom nervously—throwing in all the things that made up your gym bag. The pink running shoes, the lock, the water bottle, that baby blue hoodie.

You zipped the bag and said, "This is where we leave each other." Your face told me that a lot was running through your head. But what could we really say?

"I don't want to," I said. And that's all I said, but I had so much more.

We kissed. Wait—*just one more*. I patted the cat. You told me you liked my jacket and then I pointed at the hole in it caused by a poorly disposed of lit cigarette on Christmas Day. And then I was gone, in my car, with tears streaming down my face—Frank Ocean playing in the background:

Keep a place for me, for me.

I knew I'd see you again. I just didn't know when.

In the aftermath of what I considered to be one of the most significant trips of my life, I was changed. I was really, really changed. I looked at people differently, at my work differently, at my words differently. You cared. And that mattered. And it made me feel at ease.

Months later—they hadn't yet dimmed the lights in the bar, so when I turned my head, you were very visible and walking toward me with discernible hesitance—like a mirage of sorts. My mouth flew open and my head started shaking. And there you were hugging me.

"What the fuck?" I said.

"You should have seen the look on your face just now."

There's a reason I wasn't notified, of course. And I understand. I told you I love you and all those other things—and that matters, but I still have a lot left to tell you. As these re-visitations continue.

They might always. Just pinch me—we did actually do that one thing that one night in November—and I could feel it days later. And I think about it still—all of it.

I write these words to keep them near. And this is the hardest one to write. You've found me at a lot of different places in my life—mentally, emotionally. And there are so many other places that I want you to find me at. And you will—because you always at some point do. And I'll continue wondering. Just wondering—like, maybe. Just maybe. For all the joy you've given me after all this time. Just maybe.

DEAR SMILER

It was just last night. And you should know how many times its rung through me. Sitting with you at that bar—we kept our conversation. You said your things and I said mine. And it mattered, because my face was flushing and Jennifer turned up next to us on her birthday to buy a shot of Fireball and tell us about the woes of her life. We said cheers to her. And I think we also hugged her goodbye.

You showed up wearing that green hoodie and those holey jeans, serving to say that you were a laid-back kind of guy. That this was just hanging out, that this was just *whatever*. You smelled good, but it was a casual smell—like the green hoodie had been worn multiple times since its last washing. It was clear you weren't resting your life on this—you were here to see what happened. But there wasn't really any reason why we wouldn't hit it off. Which I think it's fair to say we did.

Leaving the last bar, it was all my doing—we locked arms and just walked. I didn't know where to exactly (or if what was running through your head was the same thing running through mine)—all I knew was that I needed to be home at a certain point and that if I saw your cute face laugh one more time, I might just fall right over.

We kissed. I let you take your time with that—lips lingering over lips. I licked, just so we could be like Elio and Oliver. And then we met, right there on the bed, falling into each other. We had sex. A kind of sex, where I did (or attempted to do) things I wouldn't normally. I took you.

We showered afterwards and, the whole time, I drew my hands across that hairy chest and watched that shiny, smiley face as it made me feel like everything I said was hilarious (or plain ridiculous), even if it really wasn't.

That night, you slept in my spot. And I let you, because I gave a shit about you. Your alarm rang at five in the morning and I cursed your name. You shut it off and muttered, "That can wait."

I threw my body around yours to feel your heat. My hand, around the hairy chest, it met you and what did you do? You touched it. You grabbed it, for the rest of the morning, until 6:15 when my phone alarm rang and I mumbled the directions for making that thing shut the fuck up.

I got up from the bed—the room was destroyed. Condoms. Articles of clothing. Shoes. I asked if you liked coffee. Then I made some, after you explained that it was too early for coffee.

You, world traveler, you'd seen a lot. And there were a lot more questions I had. Being with you yesterday. This morning. It made look again at the power of *potential*.

We lay together in bed. I sipped at my little coffee. The mug, from Stella, labelled "Let That Shit Go." I kissed your face. I kissed it again and sat on the bed, with my hand on you, to just let you know that I felt a real fondness for you—for the way you talked to me, the way you held me arm-in-arm all that way home, how you laughed when I said all the wrong things. You made me nervous.

You had a conference call at 7:00. It felt like a Saturday—which, if it had been, I would have at least inferred that I wanted you to stay with me all day long. But I couldn't. I let you go, because I had to. At the door, I kissed you three times. You said, "I'll see you soon," which didn't sound as much a promise, as a question mark.

I didn't know. Do you?

On the way to work this morning, Sheryl Crow's self-titled album played over my car stereo. "Home" came on and my eyes did that thing they've done plenty of times before. I started laughing as the eyes started welling, like that scene in *Unfaithful* when Diane Lane is on the train and all giddy about the sex she'd just had with the exotic hottie.

I got to work and my coworkers treated me just as they had the day before. They were too good, as I was still in the process of loosening up, letting the *real me* shine. If only they knew—if only these walls could really speak.

Parts of me are unsure of whether it all will happen again (I never know), but you gave me enough of a reaction—a real craving to have you next to me. I've smelled you all day long, Smiler. And I suppose, that's enough. To say we had our time, regardless.

DEAR PROFESSIONAL

I don't know if there's even anything in particular that I can say about it. Only that you were in town for a week, taking a course that was meant to make you a better manager. You were staying at a hotel, by campus. And I explained that I lived downtown. Maybe we could meet and mix passion with something a little rougher.

You showed up and almost immediately apologized that you were a little sweaty from the walk over. And I said it was fine, because we were probably about to get even more sweaty together.

You had an accent—a very specific voice. Low tone. Some sort of Norwegian carryover? Whatever the case, you were from the city where I'd just been a few weeks prior for a real let-down of a Pride event. There were ghosts that lived there that always kept me on edge. And I was on the search for something *more*—but often disappointed by said search.

The one morning:

Would you be up for a foursome at noon?

Yes. I would.

Come noon:

I think we lost one of the tops. Someone said he's at brunch. Having bottomless mimosas. I'll keep you posted as to what's going on.

You can't even make this shit up.

So, you, you showed up. And we did all the things we said we intended to do. And then we just talked—for quite some time. I watched as you put your shorts back on. I watched your naked torso and thought, I'd like to climb this every day. You weren't perfect, but that's what I liked most.

I mentioned that, one day, I intended to move to your city—that it was a personal choice I'd made a month ago, that it was the obvious next step. You said, "You need to tell me when you get here. We can meet up again."

"Okay," I replied. We kissed at the door. And then I dressed and met Sarah at the Terrace. It was Maxwell Street Days. And she and I had been talking about a pub crawl for some time. So, that's what happened. Me, in my joyful afterglow and beaming smile, I walked the streets with her all afternoon and watched as she went up to random men to introduce herself and hand out her number.

We love each other. And we feed into each other—especially as the drinks keep being poured. The dynamic duo, at it again. With you in the back of my head.

ALAN SEMROW

DEAR CONVERSATIONALIST

We'd walked to the second bar, where I ordered another vodka-soda and all you asked for was a seltzer. You'd been trying to drink less during the week, to start eating better.

You drove a good hour to meet me on that evening in September. Before arriving, you explained that you were looking for real connection, that it was becoming more and more important for you as time passed and you aged. All I could say was, "I hear ya there!"

The conversation had been good all night. I could tell you were down-to-earth and liked to talk about the deeper things—stuff Stella and I would typically discuss over wine on a Saturday night.

There was a moment, though, a space in the conversation. When my mind wandered and tried to conjure what to ask next. That's when you said, "So, when you're like out on a date with a guy, how can you tell if you're hitting it off—if you like what's happening?"

My eyes grew wide and I laughed a bit—out of nervousness. "That's a big question," I said. "But a good and valid question."

"So, what do you think?"

"Umm. I think I get giddy. Like, playful. I feel giddy when it's good."

"And then when it's over and you both go back to your lives?"

My eyes narrowed. "Then, I guess, that's when I spend time thinking about it. Letting it sit for a while."

You nodded and took a sip for your glass. "I think that's what happens for me too."

"Well, I guess, we're on the same page then." I smiled and looked around the room.

But you weren't done. "So, the giddiness, though. How often do you feel it?"

And since you were obviously being real with me, I felt I could trust you with whatever I said. In that moment, I could have given a white lie. I could have been less straightforward. But, no—you wanted me to be honest. I scratched my head and dropped my eyes from you. "I feel it a lot."

You nodded again, took a sip from the glass. "See," you told me. "I don't. I have a friend and I always give him shit about it. I tell him, 'You fall in love so easy.' I'm not like that."

I smiled, maybe out of pride—maybe it was giddiness. "I am like that. I fall in love."

It was around this point that we decided to start heading back to your car. You had no sense of direction, though you'd once spent a two-year period living in the city, getting your master's degree. Now, you resided elsewhere. Once again, you were going back to school, in the process of stepping away from the Corporate America that you had been climbing for a number of years. It occurred to you that this wasn't what you wanted to do for the rest of your life. So, you were leaving it all behind and seeking something totally brand new. I give you credit for that. I envy that.

We approached, closer and closer to where you said you parked. And then you stopped right by the dark blue mini-van and you kissed me on the mouth. Let's leave it here, right? It would make sense to just leave it here. So, that's what we did. Once we found it, you kissed me once more and boarded your Ford Escape. I told you to drive safe—you had a long road ahead and it was late.

All I can really say is that I was glad when you asked me what you did, because no one's asked me that before. It made my mind go to other places, it helped me give a name to things that I'd been struggling to label. It was real. You know, it was.

DEAR STREAMS

We'd been playing this game for some time. You must have realized how you looked at me. And I surely did with how I looked at you. Give me. Give me. Give me.

Maybe I was the one who started it—when I found out you were no longer taken. You couldn't blame me for making cause for us to make it happen. So, I kept patient. And I kept paying attention.

And, so, as a crowd of queens headed from the Pride block party to my favorite gay establishment, I spotted you from behind. I said something to Jack and he rolled his eyes.

"You'll do what you want, so I won't say anything at all."

We walked into the dark bar with the pounding dance music. I told Jack, "Order me something."

"Bitch, I have to pee," he said.

"So, do I."

I entered the bathroom and he followed close behind. I grabbed for the metal door to the stall, as he approached the urinal, and then I heard the door open once more.

It was you, Streams! And this was our time to do what we wanted.

I opened the door and you had this look on your face like, we both deserve to make *something* happen right now. I heard Jack huff. He must have stopped mid-stream and exited the bathroom immediately—he didn't want to hear it, the screeching door closing behind.

You and I stood over the toilet and let our dicks fall out. We peed into the bowl, stream crossing stream in the middle of the dark night.

I laughed. You laughed. We finished and stood there with eyes locked, like, *what's next?* You said, "I want to fuck you."

"Yeah," I said, nodding my head. "You want to fuck me?"

"Yeah, but for now, this will have to do."

My head pressed against the black wall behind me, you had me pinned and our lips kept touching. The fire ran through my veins and exhaled in a fit of rage and lust, sprinkling across your neck. For however brief, we let whatever tension out, not as an end-note, but hopefully as a sign of something to come.

We let go of each other and exited the stall to wash our hands. I stood with you at the mirror and we fixed our hair. I mumbled, "That just happened."

And you giggled, "I'm glad it did. It was about time." And you were right, Streams. I was so glad you felt the same way.

DEAR TOUR GUIDE

Do you think the headboard felt it? I send my thoughts.

The night before, you'd messaged me late. I'd just gotten in after delay after delay after delay. Considering the two-hour time difference, it was safe to say I was beat and had to decline your offer to come over and sweep me up for a little while.

For me, a new city presents a wide opening to extend or explore parts of myself that I typically wouldn't back home—the parts that might not move on as high a frequency. This trip allowed me to bring those things out—I wanted to be more open, to explain, to pay attention, be real, and be patient—at least for three days. With confidence, I can tell you that's what you got from me.

I told you I had an interview in the morning, but afterwards, when you got out of work, if you wanted to stop by and spend some time on each other, I'd be more than happy about it.

The next morning, I was taxied back from the interview. It had gone well—I liked the people, I liked the atmosphere, everyone seemed to like me. I was reminded that there's so much more out there in the world and you always have the option to seek it and find it and hold onto it for however long you'd like.

But I also had a life back home that, over the course of a year and a half or so, really became a *life*. I met people and I did good things and stupid things—a lot that I was proud of, regardless. They were things that, together, contributed to what I see as a very full period of time on my life's calendar. They were also the things that held me back from making a dramatic move. I thought about hugging the people I'd come to love on my way out, sobbing into their shoulders. I thought about boxing my things up in my studio apartment and placing them into a van that I would drive all those miles in. I thought about locking the door on a place that had become home—*if only these walls could speak*. It all presented an interesting idea to play with, but was I ready for it? To face the same initial struggles I had when I moved here. Not yet.

That afternoon, I walked to a sandwich shop, up in the gay district. I spent time at a café and read a book that I was obsessed with. I think I might have even wound up at a bar at some point, but mostly, I was laying low and being happy and being myself—stepping away from reality and exploring what I *could* be like if I were to make a really big change. I watched the people. I thought, I could find a boyfriend here. I could make new friends here. I could really roll myself into *something*.

Your kindness—or the kindness you conveyed in your messages—I think that's what turned me on first. It was clear, you wanted to connect and have fun and do the things that people who have sex do.

You were ready to talk, to actually get to know me, and I welcomed that.

I met you down in the lobby. You looked like I thought you would—shorter, older, but still youthful. Just one look told me that you led a content existence. Your weekends, they were full. Your life outside of this, it was bursting. You had found success. You were grateful. And you had a story. In my hotel room that afternoon, you let me in on a lot of it.

I told you my fears. I told you what I liked about the city and how it didn't share some of the things I disliked about the place where I was from. Then you told me what brought you here, as well as what's kept you here. You told me about your little explorations. You told me about your weekend plans.

Our sex was hard and it was rough, and then it was quiet and it was passionate. We bashed the headboard in and the wall behind it. I can still hear the *knockknockknockknockknockknock*. You tried a lot of things with me that day and, every so often, you'd slow down and you'd ask, "Are you doing okay?"

I want you to know that there's great power in such a simple question.

Afterwards, we lay together. You told me that you wanted me to come out tomorrow night to dance at this thing. It was charming. And it was even more charming when you started telling me about all the places that I still needed to see. These great, beautiful buildings that you admired. Museums, stores, the leather place that I would eventually go to and make an impulse buy.

You said, "You know, if you move here, I'd be glad to be your tour guide."

That told me that you weren't planning on forgetting the afternoon we spent together anytime soon. There was relief in that—I was bound to hold onto it, as well. When I think of that city and my time there, you should know I think of you, too. And you should know that I intend to come back.

ALAN SEMROW

DEAR JET-SETTER

I knew exactly who you were. And you knew nothing about me. But I saw you standing on the sidelines, all nicely coiffed. Quiet, observant, sexy—I'd be lying if I said I wasn't wondering whether it was me you were looking at behind those dark glasses. Something in me felt like it was.

By that point in time, I'd given up on the entire concept of agendas, so that day, I lacked one. Something like this wasn't supposed to happen—or at least I'd never in a million years expected it to. But, that afternoon, your message came through and I was given the opportunity to act. And, of course, I did. You were flying out for the week and I had all the time in the world for you.

Maybe you'd forgotten, but we had almost planned for this to happen before.

You showed up in stripes. And little flip flops, which I thought quite the choice for a cold airplane, but I would never be one to judge you—especially at the time.

You only needed to say what you said: "You're cute." From there, we took off like a fucking skyrocket. Your kiss, it was perfect and exact. The way we dropped each other's clothes, it took me back to days when I was younger. I ran my hand down your beautiful body and mine tingled back. We stood in front of the mirror. You said, "I really like this mirror." We looked into it, into each other's eyes—and kissed again. It was at this point that you lifted me way up in the air and threw me onto the cloudy bed below.

I'm picturing the throws of those final moments, when your eyes were meeting mine. I recall the sound you made—how it caused my entire body to convulse and follow suit.

This is actually happening. This is actually happening. Just pinch me.

I kissed you on the mouth. We lay together for moments—maybe a few minutes. Considering the relatively mild nature of the way we met, I'll try not to be dramatic here. But, with you and the things we had just done, I felt full. I felt like someone could barge into this apartment right now and steal all of my belongings—and I'd be perfectly fine with that.

It just happened. It really just happened.

I asked you if you wanted to shower before your flight. You seemed hesitant to take any more of my time, but all I really wanted was just that—time—with you. And I really felt it was necessary for you not to board that plane smelling of sex.

I handed you a towel and ran the water warm. We kissed again.

After you cleaned off, you told me things I'd already heard or known. We made out and you said we should really do this again sometime—that it would be fun to do this on the regular. I concurred.

You closed the door behind you. That's when time seemed to stop for just a little bit. I slowly lowered my body onto my wood floor and sat there for a good thirty minutes in my wet underwear, in the aftermath of the tornado. Coming out of it, I looked to the bathroom door, where the towel that you'd used hung. For two weeks, that towel stayed right in that place. Just because.

DEAR ONLY CHILD

I'll say that I do think we misunderstood each other, somewhere along the way, on that evening—a Friday, which I'd typically spend with friends, blowing off steam from another work week in the books. But you were new to town, and I didn't want to miss the opportunity to see what we could be.

From the look on your face, walking up to my apartment building, it all felt very promising—we both looked like our pictures. You were smiling and we hugged and made our way up toward the Capitol, making small talk. You said, "What's this place like? Someone told me it was cool."

You were pointing at the hotel with the floor to ceiling windows. It had opened about a year prior. They have a rooftop deck with two or three full bars. And plenty of wine. I said, "You wanna go in?"

"Yeah. Let's do it."

We stepped into the elevator and made our way up there. We walked out onto the balcony. And I saw a friend, Greg. I rubbed a hand on his shoulder and then we found ourselves an open spot.

You'd moved close to town less than a week ago. Where you decided to reside still baffles me—about forty minutes from downtown—cheaper, closer to work. And I felt for you in that regard, because there's so much of this city that you really should see, and that location might keep you from a lot of potential things. But I wasn't here to accept that burden. I was here to see what you were really like.

And so, you were a fan of Beyoncé. That was made clear very quickly. I concurred that *Lemonade* was an important album, that it had meant a lot to me at the time of its release. But that's pretty much all I could say to that. To the topic of Beyoncé, at least.

We had two glasses of wine and then I said, "Should we maybe try something else?"

"Yeah." You nodded. "Let's get out of here."

On our walk over to the next bar, you said that you've met a few people so far. That I'm the third. And I thought, *well, great*. We entered the packed room. You looked around and then at me and said, "We can't be here right now."

"Really?"

"Yeah, I'll tell you later."

That was fine with me—the place was way too loud and way too packed for us to get solid service. It was almost like it all wanted to give me an anxiety attack.

On our way out, we ran into Dustin and his friend, Laura. He stopped me and we hugged. I introduced you to them, which I was glad to do. Then we skipped our way out of the bar.

You huffed. "There's a guy in there. The last guy I would want to see. He like went crazy on me when I was first looking for apartments here. Sent me some weird messages."

"Yeah," I nodded. "You really gotta be careful in the underworld."

We found ourselves at the Mexican cantina. We ordered the special house margaritas. You spoke of your childhood and I spoke of mine. You were the only child of your parents. But your dad had produced three with his current wife. And your mom had produced three others. And then, out of nowhere, you asked, "How much plastic surgery have you had?"

I stopped right there. And I wondered where that even came from. It didn't require an answer, so I hardly gave one. I said, "Serious?"

You rolled your eyes and laughed. "I'm playing with you. I'm really sarcastic. Don't take it personally." Time passed and we got back on track and then you said one more thing, "How does it feel to be number three on the list of people I've met so far?"

And I looked you right in the eyes and said, "Well, I won't be number three after you fuck me tonight."

It floored you and I was glad it did. I watched as your face turned red and both hands flew up to your face. "I can't believe you just said that."

"Well, you should learn how to talk nicer to people."

You nodded and took a drink from the watered-down margarita. "Maybe that's the thing—you're just too nice."

"Yeah," I replied. "That might actually be the case." And it was a validation of sorts—it clarified for me that, on most cases, I'm not the monster in the dynamic. I'm the one along for the ride, the nurturer. The one who is trying to be open and let this thing blossom into what it should or could be.

It was maybe at this point when we both sat with the misunderstanding. I recognize now that you probably didn't mean much harm in the stupid ass questions you were asking. That it was a guard we are all guilty of putting up, to keep ourselves from feeling too vulnerable, too open.

I, too, was once the "new kid in town." I did things that now make me cringe when I think of them.

We agreed to leave the cantina from there. The walk back was mild. I grabbed your hand as we crossed the street. And, still, we could laugh and be playful, with the understanding that this might be the last time. Even though, for a hot second there, I thought this was either the first or the last time.

You said you had to piss. So, we entered my apartment. You did your thing. And I did mine right after you. I opened the bathroom door and there you were on the bed. With a dramatic running start, I leapt onto the bed like a flying squirrel.

This is going to happen now.

We kissed like we meant it—and, I'll tell you, after all is said and done, I did mean it. I did mean it when I moaned the word, "baby." I did mean it as I nibbled on your ear and huffed harder and harder as you did the same, fucking me in a fit of passion and rage.

It was distinct the sounds you made and I listened close, able to identify exactly when you were going to let it go. I called it. You came. And we kissed a few times more. The guard was now officially down. And, so, what could we realistically do with it? It wasn't shame. But it wasn't fondness either. We'd simply done what our bodies and our minds were telling us to do. And I was happy about it.

And from here, all we could do was leave it at that—two people with something in them unspoken. I wanted you to spend the night. But you couldn't. You left and, to me, it was clear we'd never happen again. I sat with it for a while—smoking out on my porch in the wee dark hours. *Were you really just a complete and utter asshole?* No, I'm convinced not. I'm convinced we had more to learn.

We won't, though, and that's okay, too.

DEAR SUNDAY

"Are you dating anybody?" That's the thing you started with.

I swiped a dismissive hand in the air and laughed. "I'm super single," I replied. "I mean, *really* single."

You took a sip of your mimosa. "I'd sweep you up," you told me. "I would if I didn't have somebody."

That's good, I thought, because I'd date the shit out of you.

You were sitting there, dressed for the day like you gave zero fucks about what anybody in the room might say or think. Finally, summer in the city had arrived. And you were coming into it with that red hoodie and the hair ablaze. I said, "Your hair looks cute all messed up."

You ran your hands through it to untidy it even more. "Can you fix it for me?"

I did my best and then you introduced me to the person sitting next to you, someone I'd already known quite intimately—Jerry. The three of us decided it would be a great idea to leave the bar for another. At some point on the way over, your body fell into mine and we walked those sidewalks with our arms wrapped around each other—like we were *together* or flirting with the idea of it. You sipped at your coffee and then handed the cold drink to me. You said, "Drink this." I made a point of placing my mouth around the edge of the plastic cup where yours had just been.

It was something I would do.

This wasn't the plan for today, but rarely is it. Mostly, I had one thing on the agenda. I'd painted these little pictures for Sarah and Stella. Colorful background with my painted black handprints on top—because sometimes I was a five-year-old in a twenty-six-year-old's body. One of the paintings served as a late birthday present. The other served as an early one. That sunny afternoon, I gripped the paintings in one hand and carried you with the other. You should know how glad I was to have met.

Of course, we wound up napping with Jerry in his bed—after leaving that second bar. I melted into the scent of you—sweet, rustled man. We slept and then, within an hour of rest, Jerry was awake moving around and so were we. Within three minutes of that, all our clothes were off—three men, naked, and throwing their weight around with each other—just because it seemed to make sense on a Sunday afternoon. And, right there, as you grew more and more aroused and your breathing grew harder, your lips met mine. You could keep them there for as long as you like. That's what I thought. You let go right at the point where I really didn't want you to.

You were planning on moving to the big city soon—moving in with the guy you loved and didn't get to see so often while going to school here. So, this was our chance. To do whatever. To be whoever. And then, to hug Jerry goodbye and leave. On our way out, you'd complain about my choice to not ride the elevator to the first floor, about how we took the metal staircase instead. You'd say you were so fucking tired and couldn't handle this. I'd roll my eyes and tell you to stop bitching—that you were such a mess (in all honesty, it was the mess that I liked in you). Outside the building, we'd hug in front of your Uber and I'd give you a kiss on the cheek.

We were bound to never see each other again. But I'd gotten to a point in my life where that whole idea no longer had to feel like a loss—not necessarily. No, it felt different.

DEAR ATHLETE

It was a quiet night—Sunday. I'd stopped in for *only one* and to take a piss. But there you all were, gathered in the empty bar, dishing and dishing some more. After exiting the bathroom, I made my entrance into your squad of people I'd known—some of them quite intimately.

I was on a roll that day and explained to two of the guys that I'd been writing. I'd been writing little letters, positive snippets about the world that certain people had shown me, for however brief. They liked listening to how I put it: "I'm happy all of that happened. I really am."

And maybe it all served as a reminder of sorts—*remember when you had me wild and feeling especially good about myself?* Because I do.

You and I never got to that place, though, I'll be the first to say we should have. We'd been living in the same complex for almost a year. We traded a few messages. That one night, I came home and explained to you how wildly attracted I was—all of the bad things I wanted us to do together. We sent those racy photos and you described what you'd do to me. You came. I came.

Your last message to me was, "Fuck, Alan."

But nothing ever surfaced from there, because I was secretly timid when it came to pressing myself into something with you that could go one of two ways. Success or no. I suppose, that's always the catch. But with you, I was more hesitant to make my way.

So, we never did. And you became unavailable, leaving me wondering, every time I saw you out, if there might ever come a day where I could make that move. And be more aggressive.

I'm not sure it'll ever happen now. And that's okay, after all is said and done.

We sat together at the bar for some time that night. At one point, a couple hands were on my dick, just to bring us all back, in our hazy field of lust. Jesse, my friend, the bartender, he said, "Put it away."

We all laughed. And I did as told.

It was time for us to go. I asked you, "Do you still live in the same building?"

"For a month more."

"Okay. I'll walk with you."

On our way out, one of the guys whispered something to you and I heard it. Maybe you should have done what he suggested, but I felt like that would be taking things to a whole other level that we needn't go to that night—a Sunday night.

And so, it was us, walking the six or so blocks back to the complex. Like I said, it was really quiet. Like the city was asleep and, we, the people who thrive on the dance and possibilities that come from it, we stay awake when everyone else can't take it anymore.

I wanted to disagree with you about something, so we began talking about childhoods, about how our heteronormative society could start to understand—how parents of homosexuals could begin to see it through our eyes. I said, "I wonder if showing a mother of a gay son *Call Me By Your Name* would make her see the truth—that we're all looking for human connection. Longing for it. This intense desire."

You brought up something about that *Love, Simon* movie that I'd yet to see. That's where my argument came in. "It's still commercialized. And I'm not convinced that storyline is reflective of the truth. The truth about the hurt of the homosexual."

I wanted to disagree with you, but I'm not sure I was even convinced by my own silly logic. But I could tell we were getting real with each other. We were having that conversation that I'd wanted to have—the one where it's two people, vulnerable and attracted to the other. I'd had many like it over the years. I mean, *many* like it. And I was glad to be having it with you,

We passed the gym where I go. We passed the tattoo shop. We didn't stop talking. We walked past my car in the parking lot. I wanted to tell you that it was my car, but why?

You turned the key to the building. We stood at the staircase. You were going up. And I was going down. We looked into each other's eyes and then retracted. We could fall into each other right now and never have to talk about it again—no one would have to know.

But we refrained. You put your arm around me and kissed me on the cheek. You told me to have a good night. And I said, "This was a good talk. I'll see you around." Which was true, I would.

There was something perfect about the way we left it. I've run into you since and, every time, when we embrace for just those few seconds, my mind traces back to that quiet summer night. I suppose, that was our time, and we can leave it at that.

DEAR FLANNEL

This summer, psoriasis engulfed my poor skin. I found myself at the doctor's and then in urgent care when the steroids they'd prescribed did next to nothing. Heighten the level of the steroid. It's out of control—over twenty percent of my body was covered in red splotches. They called it psoriasis vulgaris. *Vulgaris*, is right.

The dermatologist said something about photochemotherapy. It works for some people, but it's also $75 out of pocket per session—I'd need to do three sessions a week for three months. I said, "I can't front that. This has ruined my entire summer."

I recall the summer before, being shirtless and basking in the rays of the sun, overlooking the pretty lake. The hot tub parties. The pools. Nature. The whole ordeal served to remind me that you never really know what a person is going through. That sympathy goes a long way. To watch what you say.

You met me when it was at its worst. You were in town visiting—for just one night. Work-related. Jack and I were sitting at the bar and I was explaining to him that I don't know what to do anymore, to get my body under control.

"Well," he said, sipping at a cider. "You need to do something. You look like a leper."

We both laughed, because that's all I could do that point.

The condition didn't stop me from running—running for connection and love. I kept at it, but at a slower, more cautious pace. The one thing I feared hearing, in the throws of sex, is, "What's happening to your skin?"

I hadn't felt so unattractive, closed off, or on-guard in a very long time. But you showed up right behind us at the bar. I looked over and I could tell what you were trying to get at. I shook your hand and watched as Jack's eyes rolled into the back of his head.

I said, "Take a seat. Join us."

Maybe I was out of fucks to give. We made conversation and I was blunt in my responses. You were a professional. You were successful. You were married. You had a hot tub on the top level of your condo. You were a bisexual. And we were hitting it off.

You stood up to "do a round" at the bar. I watched as you walked away and Jack said something about how inappropriate your "doing a round" is. I replied, "A lot of things don't really matter. I like his name. It has a nice ring to it."

You came back. And then we went out for a cigarette. It was raining and I liked that it was—the mood of it. We stood in a little cove where I always sneak off to smoke. We talked more. We put our cigarettes out. I said, "Wait," before we went back inside.

And that's when our lips met. And it didn't stop there.

I sat back down next to Jack as you walked down the row to the bathroom. Jack said to me, "Are you going to go home with him?"

I looked at Jesse, my friend, behind the bar. I smiled real wide. And I said, "Yes, I'm going to go home with him tonight and I couldn't be more thrilled about it."

We had another drink or so and then you called the Uber without even asking if I was ready or done for the night. We made out in front of everyone in the room. Since then, Jack has told me that people don't like seeing me do things like that. It doesn't look good on me.

To which I replied, "Like I give a shit. I'm reacting." Some of us were born to love harder than others.

We entered the car—we didn't really need to be riding in it, the hotel was only a short walk away—but you were adamant about it. You didn't like the rain as much as I did.

I'd never been in this hotel before, but I was always interested to see. We walked in, passing all of these straight, white, successful people. And we looked damp. We looked like we were about to go have sex—you in your flannel, me in my t-shirt.

We stepped into the hotel room. And, slowly, our clothes came off. I thought about my skin the entire time. But you still made me feel at ease, like you didn't care. There was no questioning—we'd had a good time and whatever was happening to my body, it shouldn't have mattered in those moments. You made me feel like it didn't. So, thank you. It's what I needed.

We came all over. And then dressed and went outside for another cigarette. I wanted to the spend the night—it was probably two in the morning by this point. But I didn't have to. In the meantime, I let myself out to you. I told you things I wouldn't usually. I revealed what I'd only tell a close friend. I felt whole right there.

Everyone was sleeping now. And my apartment was very nearby. I said, "I guess, this is where we leave each other."

You nodded, "I guess so. Are you far from here?"

"No," I said. "I'm looking forward to walking through this rain."

You laughed and kissed me one last time. I thought about asking for your number, just for the hell of it. But that wasn't necessary. We'd done the deed. And I could walk home with a bright, shiny smile, slipping past all the places and venues that I walk by on the daily. Everything closed. Everything a little quieter. I was at peace and looking at my situation a little differently.

DEAR REMINDER

Three months ago, I told myself I was done with these, that there wouldn't be any reason to write another—because I was closing the books on a period of time in my life and looking ahead. I said, "You, Mr. *You*, you are the last one I will write about in real-time."

I take it back now. I'm not convinced there will ever come a time where I can completely let go of the notion of sitting at a coffee shop, looking around at all the students and professionals doing their work, having their conversations, on their first dates, and writing to the men who have traipsed into my life for whatever reason—and made an impact of sorts.

The story is never finished—until it absolutely is *finished*.

It's like me to meet people like you. The whole thing started on a whim. I took two days off, extending my weekend. And I decided at 4 am on a Tuesday that I deserved to make a trip. One-night-only to the city that lies below. I'd be staying at a place Jack and I stayed at back in January for a Lana Del Rey concert. I liked the vibe, the close proximity to the things I cared most to see and experience—the gay neighborhood. So many possibilities.

Traveling puts me in a place of vulnerability and openness. People drive like assholes in the city. And they honk at you if you don't move quick enough. It's a practice in patience for me. A solo trip allows time to start looking at things just a little bit differently. Because it is so different here.

The weekend ahead, it was a big one for our city and our community. Pride—it was never as big as any of the others. But someone from my past would be coming to town with the person he'd been dating and, surely, I'd run into him on the second anniversary of our first meeting. Always lovely. Always brutal. Always leaving me in a tizzy of sorts.

I drove down to the city to experience something greater—before placing myself in a situation where I couldn't ever win. Where I'd need to make an abrupt decision to simply *let it go*. For now, at least.

I got in around 2 pm. I was too early for check in, so they held my bags at the front desk and I made my way to the gay neighborhood. I'd heard about the taco place, so I stopped in for a few. It was fairly empty and the bartender treated me differently than the bartenders back home.

Sure, there was a lack of friendliness here. People didn't look other people in the eyes as often. No one was necessarily trying to impress. Everyone was in a hurry—but why?

I had my tacos and my Corona. And the bill was like $25, which is incredible to me. I walked some more and then I walked back and got the key to my hotel room. The view this time was different. I overlooked a brick wall, right across the way—I overlooked the fire escape.

This is *me time*. This is necessary. Calm yourself.

Over the last two years, I've come across men like you in the cities where I've found myself. Seattle, Denver, Minneapolis, here—right here. And I've left holding on. I've tried to understand why I do this—perhaps, the hope is that the other person feels the same way. That we met up and did what we did and left the situation slightly changed. The molecules, moved. Some of us are meant to love and fall hard.

But I've also come to realize that it doesn't matter how the other person feels, because you might never know. All I can do is come up with this: it meant something to me.

I ventured back out and hit up a bar that me and an ex-boyfriend once went to when I was much younger and much more inexperienced at the game. At the time, I thought my world was in place, but my world had hardly even started. And what I knew then was in the process of being destroyed.

I left after two beers. I walked some more, Frank Ocean singing ringing in my ears. I could see myself here—staying here, making a whole other kind of life. People never leave the city, that's what Stella told me. Here, I could see how I could stay forever. It would probably take a meltdown on my part—all the moving energy, the sounds, the cashflow. But I could do it. And I'm at a point in my life where it would make sense.

I stopped and got a bowl of poke—the place was empty. The city hadn't even started to think of going out yet. But I was ready to retreat to hotel and see where the night could go from here.

That's when you appeared. It happened fast. We were messaging, out of nowhere. You were saying that you weren't doing much. And I said the same. I said that I have a bottle of wine here and that you should just come over and we can see what happens.

That's what you did. You arrived within ten minutes, wearing that Dr. Pepper shirt and holding the bottle of red wine with the spin-off cap.

That was it—the look on your face had me right there. I could trust you. We walked up to my room, with the Wrigley Field-themed backdrop. You opened your bottle of wine and we poured it into two paper cups. And then we just sat down and talked for an hour. You had the most darling southern accent I've ever heard in my life. You told me that you really love it here—that you're glad you made the move.

You said, "You just have the cutest laugh."

You don't understand that it was everything I needed. As much as I was afraid for what might come during the weekend ahead, back in my city, running into ghosts and not knowing what to say or how to react, this was putting me at peace.

We finished our paper cups. We finished another round of our paper cups. You asked me to turn on the air conditioner, then told me about your new job, that you were thinking of getting a car, but didn't really mind the forty-minute bus ride. You told me that you have two eggs every morning, followed by peanut butter toast in the afternoon. Chicken and rice at night. You said, "It's pretty economical."

And then it all stopped, but the molecules kept floating. It was time for us to take it to the next level. You said, "You're so cute." And then we were all over each other—clothes flying everywhere. Your sounds. My sounds. A fit so perfect—lighting, thunder. It wasn't rushed, but it was intense. And I loved every second of it. How right it felt wrap my arms tightly around your naked body.

Here are we are. And you have to leave soon, because you have to wake at five in the morning for your daily work-out routine.

You told me to try the donut place downstairs tomorrow—that I wouldn't regret it. And I promised that I would check it out (I ultimately did). You asked if it would be rude of you to carry what was left of the wine back home and I said, "Absolutely not." I walked you down to the street. We hugged and I kissed you on the cheek.

You said, "I'll see you later."

Something in me knows this could happen again. A lot of me longs for it to. You reminded me of a few things—things that were overdue for a reminder. I needed to slow down. I needed to take care of myself. I needed to not think so hard, to let the situation play out as it was meant to. And I needed to pay close attention to the things happening around me—otherwise, I'd miss out on the beauty. You should know what it all meant. I want you to.

ACKNOWLEDGMENTS

Thank you to Peggy Benton, Liz Morgan, and Ben Monty for being the family I always wanted, but never thought I deserved. Unconditionally, I love you. You've taught me so much.

Thank you to Emily Zarnowski, Claire Herritz, and Hanna Herritz for your undying friendship and support.

Thank you to my darling sister, Katie. Thank you, Mom and Dad.

Thank you to Bobby Mahr and everyone at the Shamrock Bar & Grill for creating a safe space for us all to play.

Thank you to the Madison LGBT community, in all its eccentricities, for letting me in. You've made me feel at home.

Thank you to Christopher Heide and *Chosen Magazine* for supporting my work and publishing many of these pieces.

Thank you to Liz Phair, Frank Ocean, Sheryl Crow, and Lana Del Rey for the music that's been ringing through my ears all these years.

Lastly, thank you to all the men—in all their maleness—who informed these letters. Big or small, you left a mark on me. Thank you to a few men who probably should have had a space here—I just didn't know how to write about it. Thank you in advance to the men to come—next book? TBD. ;)

ABOUT THE AUTHOR

Alan Semrow's fiction, nonfiction, and poetry has been featured in over 30 publications. Apart from writing fiction and nonfiction, he is a professional copywriter, a monthly contributor at *Chosen Magazine*, and a singer-songwriter. Previously, he was the Fiction Editor for *Black Heart Magazine* and a Guest Fiction Editor for the Summer Issue of *Five Quarterly*. Semrow's debut short story collection, *Briefs*, was published in 2016. *Ripe* is his second book. Semrow lives in Madison, Wisconsin.

Made in the USA
Lexington, KY
07 October 2018